CHANGE AND SELVES

CHANGE AND SELVES

EDO PIVČEVIĆ

CLARENDON PRESS · OXFORD
1990

Oxford University Press, Walton Street, Oxford OX2 6DP
Oxford New York Toronto
Delhi Bombay Calcutta Madras Karachi
Petaling Jaya Singapore Hong Kong Tokyo
Nairobi Dar es Salaam Cape Town
Melbourne Auckland
and associated companies in
Berlin Ibadan

Oxford is a trade mark of Oxford University Press

Published in the United States
by Oxford University Press, New York

British Library Cataloguing in Publication Data
Pivčević, Edo
Change and selves.
1. Self. Philosophical perspectives
I. Title
126
ISBN 0–19–824249–2

Library of Congress Cataloging in Publication Data
Pivčević, Edo.
Change and selves / Edo Pivčević.
Includes bibliographical references.
1. Change. 2. Self (Philosophy) I. Title.
BD373.P58 1990 116—dc20 89–39350
ISBN 0–19–824249–2

Typeset by Hope Services, Abingdon, Oxon
Printed in Great Britain by
Bookcraft (Bath) Ltd
Midsomer Norton, Avon

PREFACE

WHEN a thing changes, it becomes in some ways unlike what it was. It is the same and different at the same time. Yet how is it possible for anything to alter, however slightly, without changing its identity? How can it be both like and unlike itself? This is one of the oldest philosophical puzzles, and one that is most insidious and intractable. Expressed in the traditional idiom, the problem of change reduces to the problem of the relation between 'being' and 'becoming'. Parmenides, for one, and even more notoriously and forcefully his pupil Zeno, argued that the relation was one of irreconcilable contrast, and that change was impossible.

This view, to put it mildly, goes against the grain. It seems childish, even obtuse, to question what is so patently obvious. Yet two-and-a-half thousand years after Parmenides and Zeno, the sceptical questions that they first raised sound rather less fanciful or inapposite than might be thought. The problem of change has resurfaced as a theoretical puzzle following the virtual abandonment in natural science of what Leibniz called *lex continui*, the law of continuity, and in particular as a result of the much publicized 'crisis of causality' in modern physics. The principal difficulty that presents itself is one of tracing the causal history of the subject of change. To take one well-known example, the quantum leap of an electron from one stationary state to another (yielding energy radiation) involves, among other things, a radical discontinuity of spatial properties. This granted, the question immediately arises, on what grounds, if any at all, can we speak of the same—numerically, not just qualitatively, the same—electron changing its stationary state in such a case?

Since difficulties of this kind seem unamenable to treatment in naturalistic terms, the tendency, not surprisingly, has been as far as possible to steer clear of them. This has led to scientific explanations being increasingly phrased in such a way as to avoid metaphysically committed causal language in favour of what are regarded as neutral accounts in terms of sufficient conditions; with the result that metaphysical assumptions about the altering, but none the less numerically enduring and reidentifiable, entities supposedly existing 'out there' are looked upon with suspicion, and generally tend to be guarded against in formulating scientific laws. Science, it turns out, can do nothing to explain how changes are possible.

My aim in the pages that follow, I hasten to add, will not be to try to disprove the existence of change, but simply to elucidate the conditions under which the supposition that changes do occur makes sense. I shall argue in particular that the idea of change is inseparable from the distinction between numerical and qualitative identity, and that the latter distinction, in turn, cannot be made clear without a reference to selves. If there is change, there must be selves. Moreover, selves are not just a fortuitous feature of the world of things 'out there', but their existence, rather, is part of what 'world' means.

In my inquiry I shall deliberately eschew the term 'possible worlds', which recently has been very much in vogue. The problem of change has often been associated with that of 'possible worlds', but the latter term really is a misnomer. It suggests the possibility of alternative worlds, and there can be no alternative worlds: just one and the same world in different possible arrangements.

The position that I shall be advancing, in a sense, is connected with, and complements, the arguments presented in my book *The Concept of Reality*. It will be shown in particular that the principles of 'structuralist holism' as outlined in that book can also profitably be brought to bear on the concept of change, making it possible to provide an account of how change fits into the general framework of ideas in terms of which the world can be made rationally perspicuous.

A sizeable portion of the first draft of the present work was completed during the Hilary Term 1988, when I was a Visiting Fellow at New College, Oxford, and I wish to take this opportunity of thanking the Warden and the Fellows of the College for enabling me during the three months that I shared in their table and their delightful company to devote myself entirely to my research, free from the distractions of other duties. I would also like to express my thanks to John Mayberry and Ian Thompson for their constructive comments on the various arguments presented in the book, and also to the anonymous referee of the Oxford University Press who made a number of helpful suggestions for improvement, most of which I have tried to incorporate into the final version.

E.P.

CONTENTS

LIST OF ABBREVIATIONS

GC	Aristotle, *De Generatione et Corruptione*
Metaph.	Aristotle, *Metaphysics*
Adv. Phys.	Sextus Empiricus, *Adversus Physicos*
Ph.	Aristotle, *Physics*

1

WHY CHANGE RATHER THAN QUIESCENCE?

THAT nothing is permanent is a familiar truism. The world all around us is in a state of flux and turbulence. Things move about through space and alter their features, some are relatively enduring, some fleeting and evanescent, some grow and develop for a while, then decay and perish, while others emerge into being. Change is the most striking and pervasive feature of all existence. Yet what assurance do we have, apart from the strength of our conviction, that changes take place independently of our belief that they do? Or, to phrase it differently, on what grounds are we entitled to claim that that is how the world really is rather than how it is merely *thought* to be?

It seems improbable that our intuition is deceiving us, and that the world really is at a standstill, or that it represents a non-temporal sequence of discrete, stationary states. But, strange though such an idea may appear, is it logically contradictory? It is conceivable, however unlikely, that all processes in the universe might grind to a halt tomorrow. That all asymmetrically ordered activity, at least on a macro-scale, is likely to break down eventually unless it is maintained by a steady infusion of energy is known to every schoolboy taking Physics. For the Second Law of Thermodynamics, popularly known as the Law of Entropy, envisages a steady, if gradual, slide of all asymmetrically ordered but isolated dynamic systems into ruin. The key idea is that any such system, if not interfered with or fuelled from an outside source, naturally tends towards a state of 'thermal equilibrium' in which the total energy remains preserved but the activity no longer shows any readily identifiable overall pattern. This is often taken to have implications for the universe as a whole, the assumption being that the amount of order in the universe is subject to a steady and irreversible erosion, with the uni-directional nature of this process determining the general flow of time from past to future. In the colourful phrase sometimes used by writers on entropy, the progression of cosmological time (at least in the current phase of the history of the universe) is marked by a progression from order to 'chaos'.

However, I don't mean here just a disorganized but literally a quiescent world: a world that never alters its state in any manner whatsoever; or, at the very least, one that is in every way similar to ours, except that the changes within it are all imaginary, that is, they occur in imaginary, not real time. The idea of such a world admittedly flies in the face of all our experience, and seems grossly offensive to common sense. Moreover, the supposition that in principle there could be a world entirely devoid of change seems difficult to make sense of in terms of what we know about the nature of physical reality, even if one takes on board the cosmological idea of a 'pre-temporal', pre-big bang state of the universe; a state, moreover, to which the universe is thought likely to return after its current process of expansion has run its course. A completely change-free world (whatever its structure might be) is a world where the laws of physics as we know them cease to function. Nevertheless, the idea of such a world, although it may be difficult to reconcile with what we know about the nature of physical reality, does not prima facie represent a contradictory notion. And this immediately presents us with a problem. For if it is conceivable, however improbable, that the world might never alter its state, then the question is, why does it alter at all?

The Naturalistic Conception of the World and the Sceptical Challenge

The question is embarrassing but it is not meaningless, and it is important to understand the conditions under which it can be legitimately asked. It is embarrassing because there is no clue in sight as to how one might go about searching for an answer, or by what criteria the truth or falsehood of such answers as might be proffered should be judged. It is, nevertheless, not meaningless if the reference is to the world taken in a naturalistic sense. Quite the opposite, in fact: in a naturalistic context, it may not only be appropriate but heuristically useful and necessary to pose such a question.[1]

I should explain at once that by a 'naturalistic' view of the world I mean here the world conceived as a system, or constellation, of entities and/or events and their attributes, which is supposed to be describable, in principle, in its entirety, in a third person, or in terms of a 'view from nowhere';[2] without recourse, that is, to subject-related indexical expressions (such as 'I', 'you', 'we', 'here', 'today', 'past', 'present', 'future', etc.). The idea is that propositions containing such expressions can be replaced by suitable impersonal paraphrases without the loss of truth-relevant content. 'Naturalism', in other words—in the sense in which I propose to use the term—is an extreme form of objectivism. It is an approach that is most readily associated with natural science, but is, in fact, one that is deeply engrained in traditional Western metaphysics.

In a naturalistic context, then, the question 'Why a changing rather than a quiescent world?' cannot be dismissed out of hand as meaningless. At the same time, there is no means of answering such a question from a naturalistic point of view. What is more, I shall argue that on naturalistic premises it is in principle impossible to refute the claim that in reality changes do not take place at all. One can recite what are commonly regarded as instances of change and point to the calamitous consequences that would ensue if the belief in such changes were to be suspended or abandoned. But there is no means of showing that such changes take place, or could take place,

---

[1] If, as is assumed by relativistic cosmology, the history of the universe began with what is termed a 'singularity', i.e. a space–time point of infinitely high density and curvature, then it seems perfectly appropriate to ask what set the universe going and why? (Why the 'big bang'?) The fact that this question—given that at the singularity all known laws break down—cannot be answered exposes the inadequacy of such cosmology, not the 'ungrammaticalness' of the question.

[2] I have borrowed this phrase, which seems to me particularly apt, from a book by Thomas Nagel published recently under the same title (Oxford, 1986). I do not wish to suggest, however, that Nagel himself espouses the view I am here criticizing.

independently of our belief that they do, or that the belief that
they do cannot be false. The difficulty with naturalism is that it
makes assumptions about objectivity which, by its very nature,
it is incapable of justifying.

Another reason why on naturalistic premises there can be no
satisfactory theory of change is that on such premises it is not
just difficult but impossible to distinguish clearly time from
space, and, as will be shown later on, without such a distinction
the concept of change remains obscure.

However, the main thesis that I shall be advancing in the
following pages will be that the idea of change is unintelligible
without the idea of selves, and, moreover, that to posit the
possibility of objective change is to presuppose the possibility
of a plurality of selves. Furthermore, and in connection with the
latter thesis, I shall argue that a language that contains verbs of
change must also contain indexical expressions, such as those
cited earlier, that is, the personal and demonstrative pronouns,
adverbs of time and place, etc. The intelligibility of 'change-
talk' depends upon the availability and the intelligibility of
such expressions.[3]

I propose to begin, however, by first demonstrating the
vulnerability of the naturalistic approach to a sceptical attack.
The sceptic goes beyond the question 'Why change rather than
quiescence?' by querying its underlying assumption, that is,
that changes as a matter of fact do take place. Neither objective
time nor objective change, he claims, are susceptible to a
coherent explanation; and hence there are no valid grounds for
supposing that the world does in reality alter its state.

The Eleatic Approach: A Demand for Truth Conditions

Notoriously it was the Eleatics who deployed the sceptical
strategy to the most dramatic effect, exposing what appeared to
be an irreconcilable conflict of interest between reason and
ordinary common sense. Philosophers have responded variously
to their challenge, either trying to restore the harmony or

---

[3] The intelligibility of change, of course, does not necessarily secure its
existence. For this, a separate argument is needed. See ch. 7.

disputing the existence of a rift and rejecting the Eleatic reasoning as flawed. But in the heat of the argument all too often the true significance of the Eleatic critique of change has tended to become obscured or misunderstood. I think that this critique (irrespective of the ultimate goals the Eleatics saw themselves as pursuing) might best be seen as an attempt at a *reductio ad absurdum* of the 'view from nowhere' conception of the world, and in what follows I propose to treat it that way. Bearing this in mind, the Eleatic initial position might be briefly outlined thus.

They began by in effect raising Kantian-style questions of the type, 'How are changes possible?' Or, phrased differently, with an eye to meaning, 'How are statements which are descriptive of or presuppose the occurrence of changes meaningful?' And their reply to this in essence was that in order to make clear sense of such statements, it was necessary to elucidate the conditions under which such statements could be true. Yet the latter task, they argued, could never be successfully accomplished, for any attempt to define the truth conditions gave rise to insoluble antinomies. It followed that no coherent account could be given of the concept of change, and this meant in turn that there could be no justification for assuming that changes actually occurred rather than being merely thought or believed to occur.

I shall maintain that, given the naturalistic premisses, the Eleatic conclusions cannot be faulted. In particular, the Eleatics were justified in thinking that the truth conditions which they (along with a good many other philosophers before and since) thought were necessary to an understanding of the concept of change were in fact not satisfied, and could not be. In this respect, their reasoning was flawless. But, by the same token, this showed that, if changes were to be possible, then they would have to be for reasons other than those that the Eleatics supposed were essential, and it is precisely these other reasons that we shall have to identify and elucidate.

It is necessary, to begin with, to draw a distinction between the different kinds of change. Aristotle, as is well known, identified four basic types: change in quantity or 'growth and diminution'; change in place or motion; change in quality or alteration; and 'coming into existence' and 'passing away', or—as I shall call it, for the sake of simplicity—'existential change'.[4] This last form of change gives rise to some particularly awkward and troublesome problems, and some philosophers have tried to dispose of such problems by showing that existential change, in the final analysis, can be explained in terms of other forms of change, and hence that it does not qualify as fundamental; or even that in the strict sense it does not represent a change at all. By contrast, others have attempted to show that ultimately all forms of change can be interpreted in terms of existential change, and thereby exposed as absurd. I shall discuss this further in Chapter 3. Reverting to Aristotle's distinction, the non-existential changes, according to him, all have one central feature in common, that is, they are all continuous; which, on the assumption that existential change does not count as an irreducible category of its own, means that all change is continuous.

Continuity of change was seen as an essential precondition of its causal explicability (and hence a precondition of its intelligibility). Now, since continuity, perceptually at any rate, seemed most strikingly exhibited by motion (*qua* locomotion, or change of place), the tendency was to focus on motion, and, moreover (notably in various atomistic theories), to interpret the latter concept in such a way as to include both the quantitative and qualitative forms of change. At all events, it is significant that Zeno chose motion as a paradigm case in his attempt to undermine the whole idea of a changing reality. He pursued his goal by trying to expose what he saw as the contradictions necessarily generated by an attempt to construct an analytical model of perceptual continuity. There could be no satisfactory account of change, he argued, unless it was possible to construct a consistent analytical model of change as a *continuous* process, and this was an unattainable goal.

---

[4] Cf. *GC* 319^b–320^a. (All quotations from Aristotle are taken from *The Complete Works of Aristotle*, ed. J. Barnes (Princeton, 1984)).

The Structure of Zeno's Reasoning

Zeno (as reported by Aristotle in *Physics*, 239^b) advanced four main arguments on motion, usually referred to as the Dichotomy, the Achilles, the Arrow, and the Stadium; but the first, the Dichotomy, will be sufficient for my purpose. A moving body, he claimed, could never succeed in traversing any distance, because, before it reached its destination, it would first have to reach the half-way point, and before it reached the half-way point it would first have to cover a quarter of the distance, and similarly for any number of ever-diminishing intervals; with the result that it would make no progress at all. According to a different version of the argument, the body could never succeed in completing its journey, for, given the possibility of an infinite bisection of its trajectory, there would always be an interval, however small, still to be covered. In the former version of the argument, the body never leaves the starting-point; in the latter version, it never reaches the finishing-point. The conclusion in both cases is the same: motion is impossible, because any interval to be traversed contains an infinite number of points, and it is impossible to make contact with an infinite number of points in a finite time; the reason being that the 'person making the contacts is, as it were, counting and it is impossible to count infinite collections'.[5]

Zeno takes as his starting premiss what he regards as a fundamental common-sense assumption: that a moving body travels through a continuous, albeit divisible, space. Space must be continuous rather than granular, for if, say, it consisted of certain discrete, minimal parts, it would be difficult to explain how change can occur at all, the reason being that the movement (if, that is, one can properly speak of movement in such a case) would occur in a pulsatory fashion, without anything that might help to explain the connection between the body vacating the point *A* and the body emerging at point *B*, however closely such elements might be packed.

---

[5] This is a quotation from Simplicius' résumé of the argument, in which he appears to quote Zeno's actual words. For a translation of the whole passage, see H. D. P. Lee, *Zeno of Elea* (Cambridge, 1936), 45.

But space must also be divisible, for otherwise it could not be metricized and used for measuring movement, and this is where difficulties set in. As a matter of fact, divisibility is a conceptual requirement, for if it is going to be meaningful to speak of the progress of the body throughout the whole of the interval *A–B*, it must equally be meaningful to speak of its progress through part of that interval; in other words, motion over an interval and divisibility of that interval are analytically linked. Moreover, space intervals, Zeno argues, must be infinitely divisible, for theoretically any stretch of space, however small, can be bisected. Those who think that the difficulties presented by infinite divisibility could be evaded by postulating indivisible minima merely show their misunderstanding of what the problem of change is all about.

In fact, Zeno, it seems to me, effectively dispatched the theory of minima in his Stadium paradox. The argument of the Stadium (if its interpretation as an attack on the theory of minima is accepted, as I believe it should be) may be sketched out as follows.

Two groups of four bodies each—call them *B* and *C* respectively—move in single file from opposite ends of the stadium, following a course that would take them past each other, right in front of what might be dubbed a reviewing stand, occupied by a row of four stationary bodies—group *A*. The moving and the stationary bodies are all identical in size, and, within their own respective groups, contiguous with one another. The leading members of both *B* and *C* have already reached the central dividing line of the stadium, which on the reviewing stand is straddled by group *A*, with two of its members standing on either side of it. Now, assuming that *B* and *C* travel at equal speed, their leading members will have passed the length of each other's group in the same time that it takes them to pass the two remaining *A*s in their respective directions of travel. And herein lies the paradox. For this means that *B* and *C* will have taken only half the time needed to pass an *A* to pass one of their own number, and yet all of them—all the constituents of *A*, *B*, and *C*—are supposed to be identical in size. If now we suppose that the constituents of these groups represent minima, it is clear that minima cannot be coherently thought to be indivisible. QED.[6]

Zeno's point, then, is that divisibility, if it is to come anywhere near conveying the structure of the continuum, must mean infinite divisibility. (It should be pointed out here that the kind of model that Zeno has in mind corresponds more closely to what modern mathematicians call 'density' than to continuity in the strong sense, even though the idea of infinite divisibility on which he relies does not enter into either of these concepts; that is, its set-theoretical equivalent is the set of all *rational*, rather than the set of all *real*, numbers.)[7]

Having thus set out what he saw as a minimum condition of measurement of spatial and temporal intervals, and hence a minimum condition of an acceptable explanation of the possibility of motion, Zeno immediately proceeded to show that this condition could not be satisfied. If the body traverses each unit of a space interval in a unit of time, he argued, then, given the infinite number of such units in any given interval, however miniscule its size, it will need an infinite time to cover any distance at all. Hence—given the first version of the Dichotomy argument—no sooner is the assumption that the body moves clearly spelt out, than it unavoidably leads to the conclusion that there is really no movement at all, i.e. that the ostensibly moving body stays firmly put; and necessarily so.

The Weakness of Naturalistic Counter-Arguments

It does not take much reflection to realize that, given the general naturalistic frame of reference, Zeno's case is considerably

---

[6] Aristotle's claim that Zeno committed the fallacy of supposing 'that a body takes an equal time to pass with equal velocity a body that is in motion and a body of equal size at rest' (*Ph.* bk. 9, 239^{b}33) is not worthy of his genius. The alleged fallacy is seen to evaporate if one allows, as clearly one must, that Zeno's argument assumed that time as well as space consisted of certain minimal units, yielding the conclusion that the same number of temporal units was needed to pass simultaneously double the number of the body units as half that number. Cf. Lee, *Zeno of Elea*, pp. 83–102; also G. S. Kirk, J. E. Raven, and M. Schofield, *The Presocratic Philosophers*, 2nd edn. (Cambridge, 1983), 274–6.

[7] A clear distinction between 'dense' and 'continuous' sets became possible only after the advent of the theory of irrational numbers, due to Dedekind and Cantor.

stronger than his critics are prepared to allow. The most frequent objections that are levelled against his argument are basically of two kinds, and may be summarized as follows.

One is that the argument is based on a disparity of treatment between space and time. Whereas space is presented as continuous, or rather as dense, time is treated as a consecutive sequence of discrete units extending into infinity. Small wonder that nothing could ever traverse any distance this side of eternity. But if space is dense, why should not the same apply to time? And if time (objective time), too, is dense rather than discrete, then surely the problem vanishes; for if the density of space intervals does not produce infinite lengths, neither will the density of time intervals produce infinite times.[8]

Another typical objection aimed against Zeno concerns his linking of continuity with infinite divisibility. Zeno got himself into a muddle, it is argued, because he relied on intuition to explain mathematical notions. He had no clear insight into the logical properties of sets, especially infinite sets. Mathematical continuity has nothing to do with the question whether physical space, or physical objects, are infinitely divisible. They are almost certainly *not* infinitely divisible, but this makes no difference to the concept of mathematical continuity.

Such and similar criticisms, however, arise from a basic misunderstanding of the problem that Zeno was addressing. Unquestionably the idea of infinite divisibility does not enter into the meaning of mathematical continuity. Mathematics has nothing to say on the question whether physical space or time are infinitely divisible. But, then, mathematics has nothing to say about change either. This frequently tends to be overlooked. The problem of change is a philosophical problem, and has to be tackled by philosophical means. There is nothing whatever that mathematics as such can do to help resolve it.

I shall have to say more about this in a moment. For now, it is important to emphasize that Zeno's preoccupation with continuity arose from his preoccupation with change and the possibility of change, not the other way round. He was looking for an explanatory model of change—and the result he eventually

---

[8] Cf. Adolf Grünbaum, *Modern Science and Zeno's Paradoxes* (London, 1968), ch. 2.

arrived at was that change could not be made intelligible either on the discreteness or on the continuity hypothesis, and hence, he concluded, not at all.

Given his frame of reference, this conclusion could hardly have been avoided. Evidently change could not be made intelligible if space and time were discrete. For how could the progress of a body from *A* to *B* be explained on such a hypothesis? How could one explain the possibility of numerically the same body changing places, that is, travelling through discrete space and acquiring incompatible attributes in discrete time? If, on the other hand, one opts for the continuity hypothesis, then, as Zeno was anxious to point out, things seem to become even more difficult. Thus a body moving from *A* to *B* has to pass through all the points between *A* and *B*. But if there is an infinity of such points in any given interval, then, he argued, we cannot form a coherent notion of what the nature of such points might be. Thus they clearly cannot have a size; for, if they did, then the process of bisection theoretically could be continued; and, if so, they could not qualify as basic.[9] What is more, if such points had a size, then no space interval, and no finite physical magnitude, could contain an infinite number of them, for together they would add up to an infinite size. But equally they cannot be of zero length, for in that case even an infinity of them would add up to no size at all. In short, they are neither *something*, nor are they *nothing*. Which seems to leave us with no alternative but to accept that, strictly, it makes no sense to say that the phenomenal continuum, as exemplified by a spatial interval, or a physical magnitude—or a stretch of time, for that matter—represents an aggregate of certain basic elements.[10]

---

[9] It should be made clear at this point that spatial intervals and physical magnitudes are treated by Zeno effectively on a par.

[10] Another way of expressing Zeno's point might be by saying that the basic constituents of the continuum are neither 'Archimedean' nor 'non-Archimedean'. According to the axiom of Archimedes, if *A* and *B* are numbers—or physical magnitudes of some sort—such that $0 < A < B$, then no matter how small *A* is, there is a finite number *n* such that $nA > B$. Or, phrased in terms of spatial intervals, given an interval *C–D*, no *part* of that interval is so tiny that it would not produce an interval *greater* than *C–D* if added to itself a sufficient number of times. Zeno presumably would dispute that the constituents of the continuum

This of course was the proposition that Zeno had been steering towards all along. His critique of change was intimately linked with his critique of ontological pluralism.[11] It was in particular the Pythagorean doctrine that magnitudes consisted of discrete units that he had in his sights. But quite apart from the intended historical target of his anti-pluralist critique, the linking of change with pluralism had a deeper significance. Philosophically, I shall argue, the two topics hang closely together. Thus it is not only that a rejection of the possibility of objective change almost inevitably leads to an adoption of an anti-pluralist stance; but conversely, too, an acceptance of the reality of change seems incomprehensible without a form of pluralist commitment.[12]

However, we shall have to postpone a discussion of these matters until later. What I wish to re-emphasize at this point is the principle which I said earlier could profitably be seen as underlying Zeno's critique, that statements to the effect that motion, or any change, for that matter, does take place, are meaningful only in the light of the conditions under which they could be true. Zeno, as I read him, did not wish to dispute that motion, and change in general, form a constituent part of our picture of the world. The problem, as he saw it, was simply how to demonstrate that this picture was true of an objective reality. If things really did move, as distinct from being merely believed

---

are Archimedean in this sense. Similarly, he would reject the idea (which at one time was favoured by 'philosophical' mathematicians) that such constituents are non-Archimedean 'infinitesimals'.

[11] All his arguments have this dual purpose, and those who treat them apart invariably end up by missing, or misconstruing, the point he was trying to make.

[12] The pluralism needed is a pluralism of selves (see chs. 6 and 7), not the kind of pluralism that the Pythagoreans and Classical Atomists, for example, appear to have thought essential to change. All the same, they helped to highlight the valid point that in so far as things change, they do so in relation to each other, not independently of each other, and hence that plurality is an essential requirement. An important difference between the Pythagoreans and the Atomists, incidentally, was that, whereas the latter assumed that, from the very beginning, there existed a plurality of basic elements, the former tried to explain how a plurality of elements came about by tracing it to the opposition between the two basic principles, viz. the 'monad' and the 'indefinite Dyad' (cf. Sextus Empiricus, *Adv. Phys.* bk. 2, 282) or the 'limit' and the 'unlimited' (cf. Aristotle, *Metaph.* 990ᵃ, 1091ᵃ).

to move, then surely it ought to be possible to construct a viable model in terms of which phenomena of this kind could be analysed and explained. Yet any attempt to construct such a model invariably comes to grief on the account of the paradoxes it engenders. How, then, could we be confident that motion is not just a thought but really does take place?

Mathematics has Nothing to Say about Change

Consider now more closely the mathematical aspects of Zeno's argument. The nub of the problem was that of metrication of the continuum. The point that Zeno was anxious to put across, in effect, was that in order to be able to give a satisfactory account of change it was necessary to devise a satisfactory principle of metrication of the phenomenal continuum, and since mathematics (he thought) was unable to help with this task, it could do nothing to explain change. And hence nothing could.

Now the standard criticism against his arguments, as we saw, was to say that his mathematics was defective. He became entangled in his antinomies, it is claimed, because he conflated mathematical with empirical notions. Along with his other Greek contemporaries, he failed to grasp the true nature of mathematical infinity for the simple reason that he never distinguished clearly between the properties of numbers and the properties of physical magnitudes. He defied the advocates of change to produce a criterion of continuity, convinced that he would be able to force them into a corner and expose the untenability of their position by confronting them with the paradoxes of infinite divisibility. But there really was no need for anyone to feel threatened by this sort of manœuvre. The mathematical model of continuity[13] is based on the concept of

---

[13] By the 'mathematical model' of continuity I mean here the formula that goes back to Weierstrass, according to which a function is continuous at t' if, for any real number greater than 0, there is a positive real number δ such that if (for any given t) the difference $t - t'$ is smaller than δ, then the corresponding difference between the values of the function at the relevant points is smaller than ϵ. The underlying assumption here is that, for any real number, there is always another, smaller real number.

real number and does not presuppose an infinite divisibility of physical magnitudes or spatial intervals. Nor, for that matter, can it be assumed *tout court* that the set of real numbers portrays the inner structure of such magnitudes or intervals. The setting-up of a correspondence between the real numbers and the points on a line requires separate geometrical postulates about lines (for example, that between every two points on a line there is a third point on the same line, etc.). In short, while the idea of continuity as defined in terms of real numbers may be mathematically indispensable, inasmuch as it enables us to study the topological properties of certain *functions*, there is nothing whatever that can be inferred from this regarding the infinite divisibility or otherwise of any phenomenal magnitudes. Mathematical continuity and infinite divisibility are two different and independent notions.

The suggestion, in short, is that, if Zeno had not allowed empirical ideas to cloud his mathematical concepts, all (or almost all) would have been well. This is a silly suggestion and shows a complete misunderstanding of Zeno's argument. Let me explain what I mean.

Of course there is a difference between mathematical continuity and infinite divisibility. The mathematical concept of continuity as based on the concept of real number does not either presuppose or entail the infinite divisibility of anything. Nevertheless, this does not eliminate Zeno's problem. The continuum of real numbers has no physical extension, whereas Zeno was very much concerned with trying to make sense of certain features of the extended world. The main problem, as he saw it, was how to explain the possibility of a *transition* from A to B. If such an explanation was to be possible, then it was only provided certain mathematical ideas could be brought into harmony with the world of our experience. In concrete terms, it was necessary to devise a conceptual vehicle that would enable one to make sense of the continuity that underlies events in phenomenal space and represents a precondition of the intelligibility of change. Zeno took infinite divisibility to be that vehicle, and he rode it in order to show that it leads to logical disaster.

What applies to space applies equally to time. If time occurs in a pulsatory, discrete sequence, then there is no temporal change, only a series of timeless instants. If there is to be time, there has got to be a continuity of temporal series from past to present, and from present to future. Yet the continuity of temporal change from past to present to future can be understood, it seems, only if stretches of time can be thought of as infinitely divisible; and herein, of course, lies the snag. For no sooner do we start thinking of time intervals in such terms, than we run up against precisely the same sort of difficulties that we encountered when considering the possibility of the infinite divisibility of space.

There was, then, no question of Zeno's conflating mathematical with empirical ideas. He was simply pointing out the difficulty of finding an appropriate model for solving certain fundamental problems that arise in connection with the idea of continuity of phenomenal change. This difficulty has not disappeared; if anything, modern developments in mathematics have helped to throw it into sharper relief. Consider two ideas which form a vital part of our conception of phenomenal change, but which are both called into question by the mathematical representations of continuity, viz. the part–whole relation and the idea of contiguity.[14]

The mathematical definition of continuity presupposes the existence of the set of real numbers. Now real numbers (according to Cantor's definition) represent limit-values of certain infinitely convergent sequences of fractions (or rational numbers). Furthermore, between any two members of such a sequence there is an infinity of other similar sequences. Indeed, we must assume that between any two real numbers there is a whole continuum of real numbers, with each such continuum in turn containing an infinity of other continua. It follows that any closed interval of real numbers can be mapped on to, and is in particular topologically equivalent to, any number of proper parts of itself; which is contrary to what we intuitively accept as true, that is, that the whole is greater than any of its parts. *All*

---

[14] Needless to say these two ideas alone, though necessary, are not sufficient for an understanding of change. If they were, the problem would be solved by interpreting the phenomenal continuum as an aggregate of contiguous 'minima'. See ch. 2.

infinite sets (if regarded as actually existing totalities) violate the latter axiom, but as an illustration of the discrepancy between mathematical and empirical ideas its violation in this case is particularly striking.

With regard to contiguity, we seem to be confronted with a similar sort of difficulty. Phenomenally, contiguity indicates the absence of gaps. In a perceptually continuous sequence, A and B are contiguous if they share a boundary in at least one point. For example, they may form part of a spatial structure, like a series of fenced fields in a landscape; or, alternatively, they may represent successive stages in a process, which while mutually distinguishable are, nevertheless, not discrete in the sense of being (ontologically) independent of each other. But how does such a contiguity translate into mathematical terms? The answer, of course, is that it doesn't. Mathematically we can talk of 'absence of gaps' only in this sense: that between any two real numbers, irrespective of how close they are, there are always other real numbers. This, however, does not reproduce the meaning of perceptual contiguity. It cannot do so, if only because no real number can have an immediate predecessor or an immediate successor. Thus a set of real numbers within a closed interval has a first member and a last member, but it cannot (by definition cannot) have a member immediately following the first, that is, the smallest but one; nor can it have a last but one.

So the conclusion must be that there are strict limits to what any mathematical model of continuity can enable us to explain about what we actually experience. While such a model may perhaps help to articulate certain necessary conditions under which statements about the phenomena of continuity in the actual world can be true, it clearly cannot fully reproduce what we normally associate with the idea of continuity in a perceptual context, and this, essentially, was what lay behind Zeno's arguments. In point of fact, there is some justification for saying that the realization that the mathematical models alone were insufficient to reproduce the full sense of continuity was one of the main reasons why for such a long time mathematicians were reluctant, in discussing the foundations of the calculus, to give up the concept of so-called infinitesimal quantities, and in some cases persisted in making use of this concept side by side with the more modern notion of limits, which eventually gained universal dominance.[15]

It was of course clear to everyone from the start that the purpose of the calculus was to achieve certain results that could be expressed in terms of finite numbers, or sequences of such numbers. Nevertheless, it was felt that in trying to explain how such results are arrived at, and in particular how they help solve practical problems, one could not avoid making use of the ontologically biased language of quantities, variable quantities, infinitesimal increments, differentials, and suchlike. It is not difficult to understand why this should be so. Mathematical algorithms, if taken in isolation from the context of their possible application, are just so many bits of formal machinery whose semantics remain obscure.

If mathematics raises interesting philosophical issues, then it is only with respect to the conditions of its possible application. The immediate motivation behind the invention of the calculus (at least in Newton's case) was the need to give a precise formulation to certain laws of motion, and hence certain laws of change. But the calculus, taken purely as a formal algorithm, does not throw any light on the question why or how changes come about, or what makes changes possible. Rather its application to practical problems presupposes the possibility of change.[16] It is therefore futile to look to mathematics for help in

[15] The attitude of A. L. Cauchy in this respect is particularly revealing. The idea of infinitely small increments in values of variables, according to Cauchy, is one that 'can and should be used as a means of discovery or of demonstration in search for formulas or in proving a theorem'. However, he goes on, 'le calculateur se sert des infiniment petits comme d'intermédiaires qui doivent le conduire à la connaissance des relations qui subsistent entre des quantités finies; et jamais, à mon avis, des quantités infiniment petites ne doivent être admises dans les équations finales, où leur présence deviendrait sans objet et sans utilité . . .' (*Mémoire sur l'analyse infinitésimale*, quoted in Abraham Robinson, *Non-Standard Analysis* (Amsterdam and London, 1970), 275–6). Incidentally, Robinson, quite rightly in my view, points out that Cauchy would have regarded the Weierstrassian continuity condition $|f(x + \alpha) - f(x)| < \epsilon$ for $|\alpha| < \delta$ as a *criterion* of continuity and not as a *definition*. ibid. 271 (for a definition of Weierstrassian continuity see n. 11).

[16] The operation of differentiation in a practical context merely serves to establish the rate at which the function alters its value with respect to the change in the value of its independent variable. As regards continuity of functions, differentiation does not help to 'explain' continuity; on the contrary,

trying to explain the latter concept. If one desires an explanation, one has to look outside mathematics. The 'mathematics of change' in the context of its practical application helps to throw certain fundamental problems about change into clearer relief, but can provide no solution to such problems. This I think was precisely Zeno's point, and this is why it seems rather churlish to accuse him of conflating mathematical and empirical ideas. In a sense, he was (at least with regard to the problem of continuity) merely emphasizing their lack of mutual congruence.

The Naturalistic Approach and an Invariant World

To sum up: the sceptic's questioning of our beliefs about changes conceived as objective phenomena in an objective world cannot be dismissed lightly. We have to re-examine the presuppositions of our beliefs, and in particular clarify just what we mean by 'objective' and 'world'. If to sound common sense the sceptic appears like an arrant fool, he is a fool in the service of truth.

It is important to realize that the sceptic cannot be silenced by simply pointing out that the concept of change is part and parcel of the language in which we normally talk about the world, and that the sceptic too has to make use of such a language in order to make his own doubt intelligible. If such an argument is going to work, it is necessary to show that any description of the world that does not acknowledge the existence of change cannot possibly be complete.

But how can this be shown? Mathematics obviously cannot help us in this, for mathematics (I am here excluding the 'contaminated' language of applied mathematics) is just the sort of language that does not rely on the concept of change. But neither, I shall argue, can natural science help us defeat the sceptic, for propositions of natural science, inasmuch as they

---

it cannot be understood *without* continuity. A function is not differentiable unless it is continuous, but (as Bolzano had already demonstrated) the opposite is by no means true: a function may well be continuous without being differentiable.

can be expurgated of tense (tensed verbs) are quite compatible with the idea of an invariant world.

On the face of it, this seems an outrageously incredible statement, for normally we tend to take it for granted that one of the principal tasks of science is precisely to discover reasons for changes that we witness around us. What, after all, might the purpose of science be if it did not provide, or, at any rate, attempt to provide, an account of why events happen as they do? What otherwise could it usefully contribute to our understanding of the world, or to our success in mastering it? Science is an activity of observation and experiment designed to make sense of a world that is in a state of flux. It investigates connections between phenomena that occur at different times and places and formulates theories about such connections. But in an invariant world there would be no place for such an activity.

This view is natural enough, but it is in certain important respects misleading. Science does not, and indeed can not, explain how changes are possible. Rather it presupposes that changes occur; or, more accurately, those who engage in science do so, in particular by bringing their common-sense beliefs to bear upon their scientific activity. What is certain is that we think of the world as changing. But whether the world does change objectively is a different matter. The latter question can only be settled by argument, and if there is a successful argument, then such an argument can only be provided by philosophy, not natural science.

The difficulty of accounting for the possibility of objective change, as I pointed out at the beginning of this chapter, can ultimately be traced to a naturalistic conception of the world and an attempt to demonstrate the logical redundancy of subject-related indexical terms, including the distinctions of tense. But the question is, if we are not allowed to use tense, how can we make references to temporal order intelligible? What is needed is an account of the possibility of an objective or 'clock' time, and, along with it, an account of the possibility of objective change. We of course take it for granted that there is an objective temporal relation of earlier and later, but why should such a relation be specifically temporal rather than serial in an atemporal sense?[17]

The problem, in short, is how one can make sense of time without tense. In trying to eliminate tense one is almost inevitably led to treat time distinctions on a par with spatial relations, with the result that the 'temporality' of time becomes lost or obscured, thereby depriving us of what Aristotle called the 'measure' of change.

In natural science, and in particular in the Theory of Relativity, the spatialization of time has notoriously led to some serious conceptual difficulties, which, I think, were first pointed out by Kurt Gödel. Gödel drew attention to the fact that as a consequence of the abandonment of absolute simultaneity, the relation earlier/later ceased to have an objective meaning, for an event *A* that I observe as preceding an event *B* might, with the same claim to correctness, be described by a different observer (occupying a different referential system) as succeeding, or even as simultaneous with, *B*. But if so, then, as Gödel pointed out, we can no longer assume *tout court* the existence of objective change. He reasons thus: 'Change becomes possible only through the lapse of time. The existence of an objective lapse of time, however, means (or, at least, is equivalent to the fact) that reality consists of an infinity of layers of "now" which come into existence successively. But, if simultaneity is something relative in the sense just explained, reality cannot be split up into such layers in an objectively determined way. Each observer has his own set of "nows", and none of these various systems of layers can claim the prerogative of representing the objective lapse of time.'[18]

---

[17] See ch. 3.
[18] See K. Gödel, 'A Remark about the Relationship between Relativity Theory and Idealistic Philosophy', in P. A. Schilpp (ed.), *Albert Einstein, Philosopher-Scientist* (New York, 1959), ii. 557–62. Gödel is quite explicit about what he sees as the philosophical implications of the above argument: 'In short it seems that one obtains an unequivocal proof for the view of those philosophers who, like Parmenides, Kant, and the modern idealists, deny the objectivity of change and consider change as an illusion or an appearance due to our special mode of perception' (ibid.). Einstein's own comments on Gödel's paper testify to his own bafflement by the whole problem. He writes: 'The problem here involved disturbed me already at the time of the building up of the general theory of relativity, without my having succeeded in clarifying it' (ibid. 687).

The conclusion that seems inescapable, then, is that it is not only conceivable that the world 'out there' might be invariant, but, moreover, there seems to be no means of actually *disproving* such a hypothesis. As a result one is left defenceless against the sceptic, who seems to have by far the best arguments, and this, as I have tried to show, is a situation that one inevitably finds oneself in if one elects to pursue the naturalistic approach.

2

THE BREAKDOWN OF THE CAUSAL MODEL

I SAID that the premiss underlying the Eleatic reasoning was that change was intelligible only if it was in principle causally accountable. This accords with common sense. In general we make two assumptions about change: (1) that changes are 'brought about' by antecedent causes, that is, we associate change with forward-moving time; and (2) that if B is caused by A, then A and B must be causally continuous, that is, there must be an unbroken causal line leading from the occurrence of A to the occurrence of B. Zeno's argument, as we saw, amounted to an attempt to show that the latter assumption in particular could not be sustained. It was in principle impossible to construct a coherent model to show how the causal relation operated across intervals of space and time, and that consequently there was no means of proving that what we perceive, or rather seem to perceive, as continuous processes were not sequences of discrete stationary states with no causal connections between them.

If interpreted in this light, Zeno's argument can be seen as foreshadowing what was much later famously reiterated by Hume—with all due reservations concerning the differences between their views in other respects, which are considerable. Thus, unlike Zeno, Hume holds that both space and time have a discrete texture, that is, they consist of indivisible points or moments, respectively.[1] Hume's espousal of what amounted to

---

[1] 'For if in time we could never arrive at an end of division, and if each moment, as it succeeds another, were not perfectly single and indivisible, there would be an infinite number of coexistent moments, or parts of time; which I believe will be allow'd to be arrant contradiction' (*A Treatise of Human Nature* (Oxford, 1964), II. ii. 2). The same, according to Hume, applies to space. Some commentators argue that the central role which 'temporal contiguity' plays in Hume's account of causation can be understood and defended only in the light

a theory of minima was motivated by his desire to avoid the paradoxes of infinite divisibility. But of course the assumption that space and time are composed of certain indivisible 'minimal parts' does not explain how change comes into being. For even if (as Hume seems to suppose) such minima were perfectly contiguous with each other, we would still be confronted with the difficulty of accounting for such apparently simple phenomena as an object moving from place *A* to place *B*. The point is that the mere successive occupancy of 'contiguous' places is not necessarily indicative of a change of place of a numerically identical object. Contiguity, in short, does not help clarify the rationale of change, let alone explain why changes should occur at all.

Returning now to Zeno, in one respect at least he certainly seems to have blazed a trail for Hume. For, as I indicated, his argument can be seen as an attack on an uncritical acceptance of the reality of causal connections. If—he seems to be saying—there is no adequate model in terms of which the transition might be explained from one event to another, or one state to another; if (as Hume later observed) all that we can ultimately rely on are certain associative relations between perceptions, then the question is, what right do we have to suppose that changes take place in an objective sense, and that whatever occurs in the world occurs necessarily in a causally generated sequence?

A Defence of the 'Causal Model' via a Defence of Gradualness

It should be pointed out that Zeno's argument, as interpreted above, presupposes the existence of a conceptual link between the causality, or rather causal explicability, and the continuity or gradualness of change. Now, that causal explicability and gradualness of change go together is not an unfamiliar thesis

of Hume's discreteness theory of time. (See A. D. Kline, 'Humean Causation and the Necessity of Temporal Discontinuity', *Mind*, 94 (Oct. 1985), 550–6). But the central issue is not how contiguity fits in with discreteness, but whether either of them can contribute to an understanding of change.

from the history of philosophy. Nature, it has been frequently claimed, does not alter by discrete leaps. *Natura non facit saltus.*[2] If phenomena of change were discontinuous, it would be in principle impossible to trace their causal ancestry. We would have no means of explaining what the progress from A to B consisted in, and the whole idea of change would cease to make clear sense. Causality demands gradualness, and change is unintelligible without either.

I wish to contend that on naturalistic premises one is almost inexorably led to embrace the above view; and if, despite all efforts, one fails to produce sufficiently convincing arguments in its defence, as Zeno claimed was inevitable, then one will either have to concede that change is impossible, which is the admission that Zeno was anxious to extract, or, as I shall argue, one will have to relinquish the naturalistic approach in favour of a different kind of approach altogether.

Consider, first, a possible argument for the defence. One might begin with the following naturalistically inspired considerations. Clearly, one might say, there is a distinction to be made between changes as they happen to be perceived by us and as they occur objectively. To take a fairly common example, what is perceived as a motion of a single object, on closer inspection may turn out to be a succession of rapid movements of several. Conversely, what is seen as a series of displacements or modifications of different things may in reality involve one thing only. Some changes are perceived as smooth, others as abrupt and discontinuous, for example, when apparently stable forms or structures undergo a sudden collapse and are replaced by forms or structures of a different kind. But all this, surely, merely reflects *our own way of seeing things*. Suppose I wish to

---

[2] Leibniz, for one, was a staunch adherent of this principle. It is worth quoting a longer passage from his *Nouveaux essais*: 'Nothing takes place suddenly and it is one of my great and best-confirmed maxims that *nature never makes leaps*. I called this the Law of Continuity when I discussed it formerly in the *Nouvelles de la république des lettres*. There is much work for this law to do in natural science. It implies that any change from small to large, or vice versa, passes through something which is, in respect of degrees as well as of parts, in between; and that no motion ever springs immediately from a state of rest, or passes into one except through a lesser motion; just as one could never traverse a certain line or distance without traversing a shorter one' (*New Essays on Human Understanding*, trans. P. Remnant and J. Bennett (Cambridge, 1981), 56).

light a match. I strike the match against the side of the box and the phosphorous compound at the tip of the matchstick suddenly ignites, producing a bright orange flame. What I witness is an event that seems to indicate a dramatic qualitative change from one state to another. Or, to take another example, suppose I am trying to blow up a rubber balloon, and a small additional injection of air causes the balloon to burst. The change is as sudden as it is catastrophic. In fact, such changes appear dramatic only in the light of what we perceive as stable states or structures. Objectively there is a continuous chain of causes leading from one state to the next. If there were irreducible discontinuities between one state and another, a causal account of change would be impossible; and hence all account of change as an objective phenomenon would be impossible.

The difficulty with this (and any other similar) argument, however, is that if one accepts the existence of logical links between causality, gradualness, and change, then one is equally obliged to accept that whatever threatens to undermine any of these ideas cannot fail to undermine all three.[3] Zeno, I think, was aware of this when he embarked on his critique of change through what amounted to a criticism of the idea of gradualness by first showing that gradualness necessarily went together with infinite divisibility, and then exposing the latter as an incoherent notion.

For precisely the same reasons, many subsequent philosophers who either tacitly or openly accepted these conceptual links, but wished to defend change against the Zenonian criticism, tended to concentrate their efforts on trying to restore the respectability of the idea of gradualness, in particular by trying to rescue the idea of infinite divisibility from the consequences

---

[3] The dilemma that the naturalistically oriented philosopher is faced with in this connection is sharply highlighted by the conceptual upheaval experienced in modern physics (briefly referred to in the Preface). Thus it is significant that the advent of the idea of discrete and indivisible quanta of modern quantum mechanics, which signalled the abandonment of the traditional idea of 'gradualness', at the same time unleashed a crisis of the principle of causality. The point is that it soon became clear that it was *in principle* impossible to trace out continuous trajectories, and hence the causal histories, of single particles. As a result, the whole idea of efficient causality came under a cloud; and this, in turn, raised the problem of the possibility of change itself.

of Zeno's antinomies. In what follows, I propose to examine
briefly two such defence strategies: one metaphysical strategy
originated by Aristotle, the other epistemological (yet, curiously,
still remaining in some respects within the naturalistic ambit),
proposed by Kant. Both these strategies have been influential in
their time, but, as attempts to provide a rational account of
change while preserving the above conceptual links, I shall
argue, they are both singularly unsuccessful. Nevertheless, it is
instructive to see just why they are unsuccessful.

The Metaphysical Solution: The Distinction between the Actual and the Potential

Take Aristotle's approach first. According to Aristotle, the key
to the solution of Zeno's problem lay in the distinction between
the actually and the potentially infinite. In broad outline his
argument runs as follows.

Zeno's reasoning was based on invalid premises. He
assumed that the idea of infinite bisection committed one to
accepting that a spatial interval, or a physical magnitude, could
be treated as an *actually existing* infinite set of certain elements.
He then tried to show that such elements could not be thought
of as either extended or extensionless without inviting a
contradiction; and that for this reason alone the passage of the
moving body from *A* to *B* was not susceptible to a rational
explanation. But surely, Aristotle reasons, the contradictions
disappear if we conceive of a spatial interval not as an actually
existing infinite aggregate of certain units, but merely as
potentially infinitely divisible. Zeno made it easy for himself by
demanding an answer to what was an unanswerable question.
Of course one was bound to land oneself in antinomies if one
conceived of the continuum as an infinite aggregate of certain
elements, and then tried to decide what the nature of such
elements might be. The point was that the very idea of such an
aggregate was irreconcilable with the idea of continuity. If an
interval actually existed *qua* an interval divided into an infinity
of ever-diminishing halves, Aristotle argues, then every dividing-
point would have to be treated as two separate points, marking

the end and the beginning, respectively, of each two consecutive elements of the interval in question; and, if so, neither the spatial interval nor motion would be really continuous. Furthermore, if time periods were to have a structure analogous to space intervals, then there would be no continuity of time either. All that would exist would be infinite collections of certain discrete units (no matter how small the given distance or time period), and since it is impossible actually to pass through an infinite number of such units, Zeno's arguments against the possibility of motion would hold good. But if such infinite aggregates are posited not as actual but merely as potential, then, Aristotle argues, the difficulty vanishes. It is perfectly possible to traverse a distance that is merely potentially infinitely divisible, 'for in the course of a continuous motion the traveller has traversed an infinite number of units in an accidental sense but *not in an unqualified sense*; for though it is an accidental characteristic of the distance to be an infinite number of half-distances, it is different in essence and being'[4] (my italics).

This argument is defective for at least two reasons. First, it leaves the basic problem raised by Zeno's critique of change essentially unresolved. Consider what is being claimed. It is claimed that a spatial interval while being infinitely divisible is not actually infinitely divided. But given that it is theoretically possible for bisections to be infinitely continued, then it is still not clear how a moving object does reach its target, or any point along the route, for that matter. To say that the interval A–B is not actually divided into an infinite set of elements, and hence that the object does not literally have to pass through an infinite number of points or to make an infinite number of contacts, is not to explain how it manages to make any contacts, and hence traverse any interval at all.

Now Aristotle conceivably might reply to this that the required 'push' forward is provided by antecedent efficient causes. Indeed, he explicitly and repeatedly refers to efficient causality as a source of movement.[5] But so far from helping to solve the problem, this merely begs the question about efficient

---

[4] *Ph.* 263[b].
[5] Cf. *Metaph.*, bk. 1, 983–4[a] and *passim*.

causes, and the end result is that we find ourselves back exactly where we started; for, as was shown earlier, Zeno's argument challenges the very assumption that the conditions under which efficient causes can meaningfully be said to operate are, or conceivably ever can be, fulfilled.

Secondly, the distinction between possibility and actuality is not going to be much help to Aristotle against Zeno anyway, for, given his general metaphysical approach, he is committed to saying that the possibility of infinite division is rooted in the *intrinsic* properties of the object itself; in this case, the spatial interval. The spatial interval *per se* is structured in such a way that it can be infinitely divided. But if this means anything, then surely it is that intrinsically the interval consists of an infinite number of parts; and, once this is conceded, the Zenonian difficulties will return to haunt us.

Attempt at an Epistemological Solution: Kant

So the conclusion must be that Zeno's argument survives Aristotle's criticism pretty much intact. The general lesson that emerges from the whole exercise is this: that from a naturalistic metaphysical standpoint, the concept of an unrealized but realizable possibility, in particular with regard to infinite sets, does not, and moreover cannot, make clear sense. For the questions that inevitably crop up are: What is it that makes infinite divisibility possible? Where is such a possibility rooted? And on naturalistic metaphysical premises there is little that one can say in reply to such questions without in effect undermining the distinction that one is seeking to clarify.

But perhaps the problem could be mastered by altering one's approach. All that is needed to make the actual/possible distinction work, it might be argued, is to detach it from its constrictive Aristotelian framework and provide it with a suitable epistemological interpretation. An attempt along these lines was made by Kant, and I now propose to comment briefly on his approach.

It should be stressed at once that Kant, no less than Aristotle, or Zeno for that matter, subscribed to the view that the possibility of change demanded as a minimum condition the continuity of space and time. Unless this condition was fulfilled, they all agreed, there could be no gradualness of change, and hence (in their view) no possibility of making sense of change at all. Space and time, Kant accordingly maintained, were *quanta continua*, that is, any part of space or time was itself again space or time, and no such parts were the smallest.[6] Where he deviated from both Aristotle and Zeno was that he rejected any suggestion that space and time could be coherently posited either as metaphysical entities in their own right, or as properties of things in themselves. To him, they were 'forms of our intuition', that is, our own perceptual windows on to the world, not features of the world outside and independent of experience.

Having thus situated space and time in an epistemological context, Kant believed himself to be in a position to reconcile the idea of continuity with that of infinite divisibility, without the need to postulate spatial and temporal continua as pre-existent infinite totalities of certain elements, thereby eliminating what Aristotle pin-pointed as the main source of the Zenonian paradoxes, but in a manner more satisfactory and more convincing than Aristotle himself was able to do.

Was his belief justified? He was certainly right in thinking that the problem of the structure of the spatial and temporal continua could not be satisfactorily solved in naturalistic metaphysical terms, but he was mistaken in assuming that a solution lay in trying to make infinite divisibility *epistemologically* respectable. As far as the naturalistic approach is concerned, the Zenonian paradoxes have already exposed its weaknesses. If one begins—as Zeno wearing the naturalistic hat assumed one must—with the assumption that the idea of the divisibility of the spatial continuum cannot be entertained without conceiving of the latter as an aggregate of certain elements, and that in asking how far its divisibility extended one was in effect asking what its basic elements were, one is inevitably heading for trouble. The assumptions that such a continuum consists of indivisible discrete units and that it dissolves into 'extensionless'

[6] See *Immanuel Kant's Critique of Pure Reason*, trans. N. Kemp-Smith (London, 1964), A169/B211, B254/A209.

points both give rise to paradoxes, and are equally incapable of providing any insight into the possibility of motion.[7]

Nevertheless, according to Kant, none of this discredits the idea of divisibility of the continuum, whether of space or of time. In this he agrees with Aristotle. But whereas Aristotle merely insisted that 'potentially divisible' did not imply 'actually divided', Kant sought to provide what he thought was the only plausible explanation of this by anchoring the idea of potential divisibility in the phenomenality of space and time. Spatial and temporal continua, *qua* phenomenal, he claimed, were by definition divisible; divisible, that is, from the point of view of the subject to whom they are given as phenomena. Moreover, any spatio-temporal interval, or any object in space and time, were such as in principle could be divided *in infinitum*. But although divisible *in infinitum*, they could never be actually given as infinite series. Infinite series could never be 'given' (*gegeben*); rather they were 'set as a task' (*aufgegeben*). To posit such a series as completed is to posit it as a thing in itself, and this was an epistemological absurdity.[8]

In short, Kant's solution to Zeno's puzzle involved an attempt to divert attention from infinite aggregates to infinite processes.[9] But what evidence did he have that, with regard to things

[7] From Kant's point of view, both these assumptions are metaphysical propositions, and represent what he calls 'dialectical opposites'; 'dialectical' (as distinct from 'analytical') opposites, in his parlance, being pairs of contrasting propositions for which there can be no 'decision procedure', and to which, for this reason, cannot be attached any clear epistemic meaning. They purport to say something about the structure of the continuum *qua* 'thing in itself', and there is nothing that can be known about any 'thing in itself'. Cf. ibid. A504/B532.

[8] Cf. ibid. A514/B542: 'The series are not things in themselves, but only appearances, which, as conditions of one another, are given only in the regress itself. The question, therefore, is no longer how great this series of conditions may be in itself, whether it be finite or infinite, for it is nothing in itself; but how we are to carry out the empirical regress, and how far we should continue it.'

[9] Kant, incidentally, distinguishes between processes involving what he calls 'the regress *in infinitum*' and those involving 'the regress (or progress) *in indefinitum*'. For example, the series of ancestors of someone now alive may or may not have a first member: accordingly, the regress involved here continues *in indefinitum*. By contrast, the division of a body, he claims, proceeds *in infinitum*, because we begin here not with a single member of the series and look for the rest, uncertain how far the series may extend, but with a whole given to us in empirical intuition. Cf. ibid. B541/A513.

phenomenal, the division—or what he called the 'regress of decomposition'—necessarily proceeds *in infinitum*, that is, that it does not come to a halt at any given magnitude, however small? There is no obvious reason why as a matter of fact there should be no physical (and hence 'phenomenal' in Kant's sense) indivisibles, and, as is well known, some modern physicists explicitly postulate their existence. The point is that Kant's argument in favour of infinite divisibility remains essentially *circular*. He begins with the assumption that all phenomenal magnitudes are complex, and then goes on to postulate that the division of any such magnitude always yields new phenomenal magnitudes; from which it of course follows analytically that the division proceeds *in infinitum*. But what has to be proved first, of course, is that all phenomenal magnitudes (and hence all physical objects) are necessarily both complex and divisible.

Gradualness, Causality, and the Idea of a Unitary Space and Time

Clearly there is not much prospect of putting up a credible defence of gradualness and causal connectedness of the phenomena of change—the twin concepts undermined by Zeno's arguments—by pursuing the above route. For why should not the 'regress of decomposition' come to a halt some time? And, if it does, if the basic texture of the phenomenal world is irreducibly 'granular', then how can there be a 'smooth', that is, causally continuous, transition, from a state A to a state B?

In fact, in order to sustain his thesis of gradualness and causal connectedness of change Kant came increasingly to rely on another thesis that was crucial to his theory: the 'oneness' of space and time. All spatio-temporal processes, he seemed to think, occur without any causal gaps for the simple reason that they occur within the unitary framework of space and time, which are themselves continuous quantities.

But assuming that this explanation works, there is still the problem of proving the 'oneness' of space and time. The argument that Kant offers is implausible. This is what he says. Space and time, unlike empirical particulars—he claims—are both infinite, that is, they are not limited by anything external to themselves (which they clearly would be if there was more than one of each). Furthermore, if there was a plurality of spaces and times, we would not be able to claim of any proposition about spatial and temporal order that it is necessary and universally valid, for different spaces might have different geometrical properties, and similarly there could exist different and mutually inconsistent principles of temporal ordering. All of which, according to Kant, goes to prove that there can be only one space and one time, and that they are both continuous quantities.

Needless to say, the argument proves nothing of the sort. To begin with, as has often been noted, there is nothing logically incongruous in the idea of a person inhabiting in close succession two self-contained and mutually independent spaces; even though the same could not be said of the successive occupancy of two totally self-contained and independent times.[10] Thus conceivably one might go to sleep in one such space and wake up to find oneself in an entirely different, but equally self-contained space, and be none the worse for the experience. But equally it is no great help to point out that without a unitary space and unitary time no propositions about spatial and temporal order could be claimed to be necessary and universally valid, for what is needed, of course, is a proof that there indeed are such propositions!

So Kant's reasons as set out above must be rejected as inadequate. He does, however, have one more card to play. In what appears like a final effort to underpin his conception of space and time as unitary continuous quantities, he broadens his approach and goes on to portray space and time not just as 'forms of our intuition', nor even as 'pure intuitions', but as the very material of which the phenomenal world is made up.

First, he rejects the idea of 'empty' spaces and 'empty' times. No proof of the existence of an 'empty' space or 'empty' time, he argues, can be derived from experience. There can be neither direct nor indirect evidence of the presence of the complete void anywhere in the phenomenal world. But, if so, then space and time (*qua* forms of our intuition) cannot be discontinuous.

---

[10] This objection has been most lucidly presented in A. M. Quinton, 'Spaces and Times', *Philosophy*, 37 (1962), 130–47.

For if they were discontinuous—if they had a granular texture—one would have to allow the possibility of there being gaps between the respective spatial regions, or time periods, devoid of all phenomenal material, and this is not an epistemologically sustainable proposition. Whereas the phenomenal material may be unequally distributed across space, there is no area from where it is completely absent.

In short, we are presented with a picture of a universal substance filling up the whole of the phenomenal universe, and once this position is reached—as Aristotle, incidentally, had already noted[11]—there is no alternative to interpreting all changes in terms of *alterations* of states of that one substance. This is precisely the interpretation that Kant opts for.[12] Having begun by affirming that space and time are 'forms of our intuition' and not properties of things in themselves, he went on to argue that, inasmuch as they are indistinguishable from specific items in space and time, they are given to us as 'pure intuitions' (not as concepts), and eventually ended up by in effect according them the status of an all-pervading and imperishable substratum of phenomenal change.

The Collapse of the Anti-Zenonian Argument

But does this help to answer Zeno's sceptical challenge regarding the causal accountability of change? It is clear, I think, that it does not. On the face of it, some difficulties seem to disappear. Thus the existence of an enduring and all-pervading substance—if such a substance does exist—seems at least to ensure that no bodies are mysteriously emerging from, or 'leaping' through, the void. In addition, the problem of how a body can change its place while still remaining the same body is (so it seems) exposed as a pseudo-problem, for a change of place is shown to be only a modification of one and the same omnipresent substance which moves nowhere at all.

---

[11] Cf. GC 314ᵃ.

[12] This, at any rate, is the picture that emerges from Kant's discussion of the 'Analogies of Experience' in the *Critique of Pure Reason*.

Yet clearly the key problem of causal accountability remains untouched by all this. For even if the notion of a universal substance as a self-identical substratum of change were free from theoretical difficulties, which it is not (as will be shown in the next chapter), this would still leave open the question of just what the change of states of such a substance consists in. If all processes can in principle be subdivided into an infinity of states, then it is not clear how the immediate predecessor of any state can ever be identified; and indeed how the possibility of any alteration can be explained at all.

This, then, is the problem for Kant's (and any other similar) theory. If one wishes to claim that changes are produced by efficient causes, one cannot at the same time deny that they must have an in principle traceable ancestry. But how can their ancestry be traced? If the set of causal conditions forms a continuum—which it must do if the change is to be gradual—then the difficulty is to know just how we do advance from one state to the next: which is precisely the problem that Zeno highlighted. What is called into question here, in short, is the very basis of the belief in the causal accountability of change.

But perhaps there is no need to refer to causal relations anyway. Why, one might ask, should a causal account of change be necessary? A main premiss of Zeno's critique of change is that, if a causal account of change is not possible, then no rational account of it is possible, and both Aristotle and Kant seem to have subscribed to this view. But in this, surely, they were mistaken.

The Elimination of Causality from Scientific Laws

Consider some examples of treatment of change from natural science. Scientific explanations are couched not in terms of efficient causes but in terms of reasons that are derived from certain laws. In order not to stray too far from Zeno's examples, let us for the time being confine ourselves to the simplest form of change, i.e. change of place. There is a well-known story according to which Galileo first made his discoveries about the acceleration of falling bodies while watching a lamp swing back and forth in the Cathedral of Pisa. He used his pulse to time the oscillations, and found that the lamp took the same time to complete the oscillation irrespective of the amplitude of the swing. Moreover, lamps of different size and weight behaved in the same manner. He confirmed his observation by rolling balls down an inclined plane and measuring their speed. All this contradicted Aristotle's assumption that heavier bodies fall faster. The ratio between distance and time in free-falling bodies, Galileo found, was always the same, regardless of the latter's weight or density; and the same applied to the rate of acceleration.

The crucial feature of this description was that it did not involve any mention of efficient causes. In a broader context, Galileo admittedly talked of acceleration being produced by the action of a 'force'. But a reference to an acting force was not needed in the actual formulation of his law. Later on Newton, too, spoke occasionally of force as the 'causal principle of motion and rest', and drew a distinction between the force of inertia (supposedly inherent to the body) and the 'impressed' forces acting on a body from outside. Thus, according to the First Law of Motion, a body continues in the state of rest or uniform motion, unless it is 'compelled by impressed forces to change that state'. Yet, as has often been pointed out, this appeal to forces as causes of motion and rest is really unnecessary and can be dispensed with by suitably rephrasing the laws in question. According to the Second Law of Motion, the force acting on a body is proportional to the product of that body's mass and acceleration. Although Newton here speaks of the force merely as being proportional to the product of mass and acceleration, it is clear that for scientific purposes the latter could be treated as its definition. If this is accepted, then the First Law can be appropriately reformulated in the spirit of such a definition, and it is no longer necessary to appeal to forces as efficient causes.

There is never any logical need in formulating scientific laws to appeal to causality. A distinction is sometimes drawn between 'causal' and 'statistical' laws, but this distinction is more of historical than theoretical interest. A causal law is supposed to exhibit certain necessary connections between phenomena, such that given certain initial conditions (the initial conditions to be defined essentially in terms of the positions and momenta of the relevant bodies or points of mass) accurate predictions can be made about the future behaviour of such bodies or points of mass in any particular instance, with the accuracy of prediction depending upon the degree of accuracy of the description of the initial conditions. The laws of classical mechanics (such as the laws of motion referred to earlier) are usually described as causal in this sense. A statistical law, on the other hand, is said to express certain sequential regularities, usually, though not necessarily, based on observation of a large number of cases, and allowing prediction, with a specific degree of likelihood, of certain patterns of phenomena rather than the behaviour of individual particles. It is probabilistic rather than categorical and universal. The laws of quantum mechanics are said to fall in the latter category. But the distinction is largely spurious, for all laws in effect depict, or purport to codify, the regularities of certain sequences of phenomena, and, as Hume (reviving in this respect the spirit of Zeno's own arguments) showed, there can be no proof of the existence of necessary connections anywhere (outside logic, that is).

Explanations in Terms of Sufficient Conditions

A scientific law, on its own, explains nothing: it merely states the relationship between certain variables. A law can be used for the purposes of explanation, but the nature of such an explanation essentially consists in exhibiting the *logical* relationships between certain states of affairs rather than demonstrating the existence of certain ontological causal links between certain events or classes of event.

Suppose the fuse in my house blows. I wish to know why, and after making a few tests find that the same thing occurs each time I switch on the powerful new electric saw I have acquired. If I am superstitious I might attribute magic powers to electric saws. However, further tests reveal that other appliances can have the same effect, depending upon how many of them happen to be plugged into the system at any given time. Of course, this too could be just coincidence. Then it slowly comes back to me what I had been taught in school physics about the flow of current in electric wires. The strength of the current in the circuit, according to Ohm's Law, is equal to the ratio between voltage and resistance. Let us assume this holds universally. Then it follows (logically follows) that if several appliances are switched on in parallel, such that the resistance in the circuit is lowered, the strength of the current will increase. This in turn will result in an increase of wattage (or rate of energy) in the fuse wire and the wire will melt. An explanation of what has happened is now ready to hand. If asked, I can say simply that the fuse blew because the circuit was overloaded.

Appearances to the contrary, the explanation given does not rely on efficient causes. It does not need to. Even though the law in this instance is asserted in a categorical form instead of—as might be more appropriate—being expressed in probabilistic terms, efficient causes need not feature in the account of what has happened. For all that is required is to show that the law plus the appropriate minor premiss (or premisses) stating the relevant evidence provides the logically sufficient conditions of the truth of the proposition reporting the event in question (the explanandum). It is like saying that 'this piece of metal attracts iron filings' is true because this piece of metal is a magnet, and all magnets attract iron filings; or that 'Socrates dies' is true because Socrates drank hemlock, and drinking hemlock is lethal. The explanation, in short, reduces to a categorical syllogism in which the conclusion is logically entailed by the premisses.

Notice, though, that although the conclusion in such cases is established by the premisses, it is not uniquely established by the premisses. The overloading of the circuit in given circumstances is sufficient for the fuse to blow, although the fuse might blow for any number of other reasons as well. Similarly, this piece of metal might attract iron filings even if it was not a magnet in any established technical sense. Socrates does not have to drink hemlock in order to die, although drinking hemlock suffices. What conditions will qualify as sufficient in a given case will obviously depend upon the kind of theoretical assumptions that we start out with. Such assumptions are subject to constant revision: they are modified, changed, or replaced by different ones in the light of new evidence, or as a result of rearrangements and modifications elsewhere in the complex network of our beliefs, and our explanations inevitably will change accordingly.

As it happens, the explanation need not even be phrased in terms of sufficient conditions. For if the law or laws that serve us as our principal theoretical premisses are stated in probabilistic terms, then obviously the relationship between the premisses and the conclusion will change accordingly. Probabilistic premisses warrant only probabilistic inferences. In consequence, we shall no longer be able to say that Socrates died because he drank hemlock, but merely that his drinking hemlock is very likely to have led to his death; or that in the circumstances the most probable explanation of his death is the fact that he drank hemlock. Similarly given a probabilistic formulation of Ohm's Law, we shall have to say not that the fuse blew because the circuit was overloaded, pure and simple, but merely that in the circumstances this was the most likely, and—given our attachment to physics—most acceptable explanation of why it failed as it did.

In short, the explanation is given in terms of reasons that *contextually seem most appropriate*. These reasons do not necessitate the outcome: they merely make it probable. The predicted event (such as Socrates' death or the fuse blowing) may but need not materialize. If it does not, this does not necessarily call for a change of the theoretical premisses upon which our reasons happen to be based, although, if this occurred often enough, it might.

Counterfactual Situations and the Causal Law

Now the most obvious objection to the above view, and one that is most frequently heard, is the following. Surely, it is said, scientific explanations are not confined simply to supplying reasons for what actually occurs, but also for what fails to occur, or might or would occur if the appropriate circumstances prevailed. Indeed, unless they could be extended to potential instances and potential situations, they would be of little practical value. Thus we want to say not just that the overloading of the circuit is sufficient to explain the fuse blowing, but that the fuse would not have blown if the circuit had not been overloaded. Similarly, other things being equal, Socrates would not have died if he had not drunk hemlock. In short, we normally assume that two consecutive events can be connected in such a way that, unless the antecedent event occurred, the consequent event would not have occurred either, and this is precisely what is meant by the cause–effect relationship. If such a connection did not exist, or was in principle undetectable, all our efforts designed to forestall certain events by eliminating or neutralizing their 'causes' would be meaningless. We assume that the fuse—unless other 'causes' intervened—could be kept functioning by keeping the amperage in the circuit within certain limits, and that Socrates would have stayed alive if he had not drunk the poisonous potion, or if an appropriate antidote were to have been administered to him in time.

The weakness of this objection lies in its heavy reliance on the 'other-things-being-equal' proviso. The idea of a necessary connection is explained by postulating the possibility of recurrence of exactly similar situations. But to say that in an exactly similar situation necessarily an event *B* follows an event *A* is a tautology which says nothing about their causal relationship. In reality of course no two situations are exactly similar, and this means that one cannot say with certainty that a given event, or series of events, would not have occurred if certain other, antecedent events, had not taken place. All we can do is to make intelligent guesses, basing such guesses upon certain theoretical premises relating to what might, or is likely, or 'ought', to occur under roughly similar circumstances. In short, there is no fail safe criterion whereby one might decide in respect of any given two consecutive events whether they are necessarily connected. But, then, the question arises of on what grounds one can meaningfully say of any event that it necessarily depends for its occurrence upon some other antecedent event, or indeed how one can give meaning to the assumption that *anything occurs at all.*

Causal Accountability and the Possibility of Change

This brings us back to the problem with which we started. Normally we take it as a matter of course that changes occur objectively, independently of whether they are believed to occur. But what are the conditions of their occurrence? Or, to rephrase the question in terms of meaning, what makes· the assertion that they occur significant? This was the question that interested Zeno, and the answer that he came up with, as we know, was that no clear account could be given of the assumption that changes do take place, because no coherent account could be provided of the conditions under which statements descriptive of, or presupposing, changes could be true. Notice, incidentally, that Zeno's argument automatically transfers to time: if changes are no part of an objective world, then neither is time.

Zeno's interpretation of the conditions of significance of change claims, however, is limited by what I take to be his overall frame of reference. The guiding premiss underlying his analysis, as I see it, is that if changes objectively take place, then they must in principle be causally accountable. But causal accountability—this is the substance of his argument—depends on the infinite divisibility of spatial and temporal continua, and infinite divisibility is an incoherent notion. It should be borne in mind that causal accountability here means essentially accountability in terms of efficient causes.

Astonishingly enough, both Aristotle and Kant, rather than challenging Zeno's premisses, basically accepted his frame of reference and concentrated their efforts on attempting to rehabilitate the idea of infinite divisibility by showing that if adequately interpreted it could be made proof against Zeno's criticism. Thus Aristotle, as we saw, argued that phenomenal continua, though potentially infinitely divisible, are not actually infinitely divided. Kant, for his part, claimed that this distinction could be made to work only from an epistemological standpoint, specifically, in the spirit of his own 'transcendental idealism'. If infinite divisibility attached to things in themselves, then one would indeed have no choice but to accept that such things existed as infinite aggregates of certain elements, with all the difficulties that that entailed. But if things were considered under the conditions that make knowledge possible, then, he claimed, the situation was quite different, for in such a case all that could be significantly asserted was the possibility of an infinite 'regress of decomposition', that is, the possibility of a process initiated by an epistemic subject being (theoretically) continued *in infinitum*.

But these were pseudo-solutions. Both Aristotle and Kant were hamstrung in their respective analyses by the exaggerated importance they tended to attach to efficient causality, even though Aristotle himself coined a set of concepts, in particular by drawing a distinction between four different types of cause (material, formal, efficient, and final), which should have enabled him to deal more effectively with Zeno's challenge. In my view, it was precisely this tendency to place undue stress on efficient causality that inspired obsessive preoccupations with spatio-temporal continuity and led to desperate efforts to construct a serviceable mathematical model of phenomenal change. This, as Zeno showed, was a doomed enterprise. Mathematical models cannot help to explain how change is possible or why it occurs, and modern algebraic theories of continuity so far from undermining Zeno's arguments merely help to confirm Zeno's original insight.

Yet the problem seems to be that, if we give up the traditional causal model of change involving the idea of certain antecedent causes 'bringing about' certain effects, and, in describing the phenomena of change, confine ourselves exclusively to investigating the sufficient conditions, then it is no longer clear that we are talking about change at all. An account in terms of sufficient conditions, strictly, is not a causal account at all. We associate causes with irreversible sequences in time. But in an account in terms of sufficient conditions time in effect fades out of the picture. A considerable amount of philosophical debate has revolved around the question of the possibility of 'backward causation', that is, whether present events can be significantly regarded as causes of past events. But if causation is understood in the ordinary sense, as involving an asymmerical temporal relation between causes and their effects, then the thesis of backward causation is plainly nonsense; whereas, if causation is interpreted in terms of sufficient conditions, then the thesis becomes trivial. Present events evidently can with as much justification be held to be the sufficient conditions of past events, as past events can be held to be the sufficient conditions of present events. The point is that the interpretation of causation in terms of sufficient conditions creates a perfect symmetry between causes and effects, and is entirely compatible with a world from which time and change are absent.

3

ATTRIBUTIVE AND EXISTENTIAL CHANGE

IT is now necessary to look more closely at the logical grammar of attribution of change. The substance of the Zenonian argument, as we saw, was that the conditions of a significant attribution of change are not fulfilled, because there can be no unequivocal, let alone reliable, criteria of causal continuity, and hence no coherent notion of the conditions under which such an attribution could be said to be true. But why, one might ask, does one have to accept the Zenonian premisses? Why should one have to tie the meaningfulness of statements about change to their truth conditions? And why in particular should such truth conditions have to include the criteria of causal continuity? To insist on the criteria of causal continuity is like asking for the criteria whereby one could establish that a perceptual object, say this lamp on my desk, is causally continuous with its earlier existence before one can meaningfully refer to it as a spatio-temporal particular inhabiting an objective world out there. It is an absurd demand. What we should be focusing on instead are the conditions under which the very question about such criteria can be intelligibly asked, and, if we do this, we shall soon discover that the possibility of referring to enduring external objects is included among such conditions. And the same, surely, applies to change. One cannot rationally insist that a definition be produced of the criteria of causal continuity of change before the existence of objective change can be meaningfully asserted, if one has to posit the possibility of objective change before one can even begin to ask meaningful questions about the criteria of causal continuity. Any scepticism in such cases is self-defeating, for in the end one is reduced to presupposing what one is trying to question.

However things are not quite so simple, and, as we shall see presently, there are considerable difficulties in clarifying just what is involved in attribution of change, even if we do set aside the question of the criteria of causal continuity. One particularly thorny problem is that of existential change, that is, change involving not just an alteration of attributes of the subject of change, but the latter's demise or emergence into being. What kind of phenomenon does this represent? Is it a real change, and of what, if anything, can it be properly predicated? Another problem is whether being past, present, or future, or even 'having' a past, present, and future, can properly be regarded as 'attributes' of some ontological items that are subject to change; or, if they are not attributes of anything, how exactly should they be interpreted? Speaking generally, what is required is a clarification of the relation between change and tense.

The Idea of an Identical Subject of Change

Let us begin with some preliminary observations about the way we normally talk about change. Ascribing change normally means ascribing it to someone or something that undergoes, or endures, or experiences, change. Moreover, the assumption is made that a succession of different, indeed mutually incompatible, predicates can be ascribed to the same subject over time. This sheet of paper was blank, smooth, and clean when I took it out of the box only a little while ago, whereas now it is scribbled on, slightly creased, and has finger-marks around the corners. Once upon a time the green sweater I am now wearing was new and had a bright satin sheen, but now looks tatty and crumpled, and has patches at the elbows. All changes involve acquisition of new predicates, but not all acquisitions of new predicates necessarily involve changes or modifications of the · things concerned. The bookcase in my room is to the left of my desk. But if I move the bookcase to the opposite corner of the room, my desk as well as the bookcase will have acquired new relational predicates, although the desk itself will not have been involved in the operation in any way. I change if I become ill, or bald, or adept at playing tennis, but not if I become a father-in-law as a result of my son's marriage. Such cases are clearly different. Yet different though they are, they are not always or necessarily different. Thus the distinction between the change 'in the subject', or, as it is sometimes called, the 'real' change, and what appears to be a purely external 'relational' change, does not work in a monist ontology, where all changes are real changes, inasmuch as they are all ultimately attributable to a single universal subject.[1]

Nevertheless, the fundamental assumption in all cases involving ascription of change (*qua* change of attributes)—I shall come to the problem of existential change in a moment—is that there is an enduring, identical subject of change. This seems so obvious a requirement; so trite, in fact, that it hardly bears mentioning; yet the idea of an 'identical subject' is fraught with problems and difficulties. For the immediate question arises, 'identical' in what sense exactly? What are the enduring features of the subject of change? Does the subject retain its identity merely in virtue of preserving its 'essential' as distinct from its 'inessential', qualities, or is it necessary for it to satisfy the additional condition of numerical uniqueness? What is the criterion for distinguishing between numerical, or existential, uniqueness, and qualitative sameness? Where is this distinction rooted?

The importance òf this distinction in any explanation of change cannot be overstressed. Yet no clear account of it can be provided within the naturalistic context, and as a result the concept of a subject of change remains obscure. In fact, as we shall see presently, in naturalistic ontologies the hunt for the basic subject, or subjects, of change usually becomes a hunt for the basic subject, or subjects, of predication that in essence do not change at all.

---

[1] The capacity for a 'real', as distinct from a mere 'relational' change, is sometimes seen as a criterion of the actual existence of the subject of change. For example, Peter Geach ('What Actually Exists', *Proceedings of the Aristotelian Society*, supp. vol. xlii (1968), 7–16) argues along these lines. However, my principal objective here is not to attempt to answer the question 'What does actually exist?' (which I think is the wrong question to start with, anyway) but to elucidate the assumptions underlying the concept of change in general.

Things and Events

Let us, first, say a few words about the distinction between things and events which the logical assumption of an enduring subject of change is sometimes thought to make necessary. Things change, it is argued, events don't. Unlike events, things have no temporal parts; rather they are 'wholly present' throughout their lifetime. They don't forfeit their identity as a result of shedding old or acquiring new attributes. The pen with which I am now writing is the same pen that I bought in a stationery shop some weeks ago, although its chemical ink has nearly run out. The tree that has shed its leaves is still the same tree. Socrates in his old age is the same individual as Socrates in his youth. By contrast, events don't persist through time. They literally consist of temporal parts, and hence cannot significantly be said to change. Change requires invariance as well as a variation through time.

However, there are problems in deciding what items qualify as 'invariant', and in what sense. Traditionally, invariance has been associated with substantival entities, but there is a sense in which invariance (of varying duration) can be attributed to a much broader range of items. Some philosophers who have found the concept of a substantival entity too restrictive have therefore deliberately used the more broadly based technical term 'continuant'. Others have preferred to use an extended concept of a 'thing'; classifying among 'things' not just physical objects and persons, but any systems, collectives, or corporate entities such as nations, churches, firms, associations; anything that can be said to be capable of possessing, non-simultaneously, incompatible attributes. Committees and orchestras are thus described as 'things', although the same is said not to be true of committee meetings or orchestra performances. In short, the criterion for calling one type of item a 'thing' and another an 'event' is said to consist in whether the item in question can be meaningfully described as 'changing', while maintaining its overall identity.[2]

---

[2] Cf. D. H. Mellor, *Real Time* (Cambridge, 1981), 104 ff. and *passim*.

This is not a very reliable distinction. Thus events as well as things often alter their features without forfeiting their identity. A concert performance may start off well, then flag and lose sparkle as it goes along, or even veer off the rails altogether and end as a fiasco. Committee meetings tend to be long and boring, but occasionally they may contain moments of excitement or light relief. Public speeches fluctuate in quality and their impact on the audience often varies during the course of their delivery. These are real changes. If the aim of the thing/event distinction is to reinforce the belief that things rather than events are ontologically basic, and that the existence of change demands that this should be so, then it clearly fails in its purpose.

As it turns out, as far as the problem of accounting for the possibility of change is concerned, the distinction does not make a great deal of difference anyway, for, as we shall see presently, on either hypothesis—whether we take things or events as basic—the problem of change, in a naturalistic context, proves intractable.

The Ontology of Things and the Phenomenon of Existential Change

The easiest way to show this is to consider the phenomenon of existential change, and the way this phenomenon generally tends to be handled from a naturalistic standpoint. If a change of some sort takes place, the natural question to ask is: *what does change?* Yet it is not always clear how, if at all, such a question can be answered, if only because not all empirically observed changes seem to be changes of attributes of enduring things. Socrates changes as he grows older, but endures as the same individual, and so does the plum tree at the bottom of my garden. But when the weather changes, one meteorological state is replaced by another; there is no enduring entity that changes its attributes. On what grounds, then, are we entitled to speak here of a 'real' change taking place? Or take a different example. The sofa, as everyone knows, can be turned into a bed, and the bed back into the sofa. But how can this be? The sofa is the sofa and the bed is the bed. They are by definition different. The sofa, of course, is subject to change in other ways. It gets old and scruffy and coffee-stained, and gets its upholstery replaced. It acquires new and sheds old attributes throughout its wretched existence. I don't mean that kind of change. I mean the kind of change whereby the sofa *ceases to exist* as a sofa and becomes something quite different; a transformation by death, if you like. What exactly does happen when the change is such that it results in the destruction of the subject of change?

We inhabit a world of finite, perishable things, in which birth and death are commonplace. Entities emerge into life and vanish from existence; and frequently, as in the case of persons, we keep a careful record of their life-span. We use phrases such as '*A*'s birth', or 'The birth of *A*', and '*A*'s death', or 'The death of *A*', in much the same way as '*A*'s health' or 'intelligence' or 'height', as if they all were logically on a par. Yet, unlike health, intelligence, or height, birth and death strictly cannot be predicated of anything. The subject of change does not acquire a new attribute by going out of existence; it simply ceases to be. Similarly, when an entity emerges into being, it does not acquire the 'attribute' of existence; rather, by virtue of emerging into existence it constitutes itself as a subject of attributes.

So how should existential change be explained? How is it possible for a subject of change to be at one time, and not to be at another? If, in talking about the coming into being or going out of existence of a given object, that is, about its existential change, we are not really talking about that object, what is it that we are really talking about? The question is baffling to common sense, and, as is well known, some philosophers have tried to resolve the puzzle by denying that existential change can be attributed to real substances, while others have gone farther still and have disputed that existential change in the literal sense of the term can be significantly said to occur at all.

Let us consider the first and weaker of these two theses. The argument is that what appears as an existential change of one entity is merely a change of state of another. If I put a match to this piece of paper and the paper goes up in smoke, it is not this paper that changes; rather it is the material of which the paper is made that changes its state. If the paper literally became a cloud of smoke, it would change its identity, which is a logically impossible feat. The alchemists are said to have attempted to discover a method for converting lead into gold, but this was not just an empirical but a *logical* absurdity. Lead can as little be converted into gold as water can be converted into wine. If by some miracle the alchemists had succeeded in their enterprise, they would not have converted lead into gold, but rearranged the structure of the atomic material of which the lead they experimented with was made up in such a way that its chemical properties became altered.

One conclusion derived from this (as we already know from our discussion of Kant) was that in reality there was only one subject of change—the one universal substance underlying all appearances—and that all changes were reducible to alterations of state of that single substance, which was indestructible and whose 'quantum in nature is neither increased nor diminished'.[3] This idea became enshrined in the familiar conservation laws of physics, and it is interesting to contemplate that such laws originated not from any empirical observations but were on the contrary inspired by purely a priori reflections about the nature of change.

Is the Universal Substance Subject to Change?

However, there are obvious conceptual difficulties associated with the above view. To begin with, if all changes, as is claimed, ultimately represent alterations of state of one and the same stuff, what might be the nature of such a stuff, and how could it be identified? Let F be its defining quality. Then the immediate problem arises of how F can alter its state to produce the perceptual variety of the phenomenal world without forfeiting its own identity. Notice that it is not enough to reply to this by simply pointing out that there are substances, like water, for example, that can alter their mechanical properties without changing their chemical composition. Liquid water, steam, snow, and ice, while having certain basic chemical properties in common are, nevertheless, four different types of material. I can take a shower with liquid water but I cannot use

---

[3] Cf. *Critique of Pure Reason*, A182.

it to build an igloo, and snowmen cannot be built with steam. That these different materials share certain chemical properties does not necessarily mean that there must be a certain common and *independently identifiable* stuff of which they are modifications. It is important that the distinction between common properties and common stuff should be kept clearly in mind. It is conceivable that all existents should have certain qualities in common (what are traditionally referred to as the 'primary qualities'), without this necessarily implying that they all must have a common origin; or indeed that there should be such a thing as a universal substance at all.

The Impossibility of Universal Substance

In fact, it is possible to go further still and argue that no such 'common stuff' could exist anyway, for this reason. If a common stuff of the F sort were capable of independent existence (rather than F being merely a feature shared by different things or substances), then the question that would have to be answered is how such a stuff could generate different kinds of material. As with lead and gold, one would have to postulate something yet more basic which could be modified into different substances; and this would mean that F could no longer be treated as the fundamental quality one originally assumed it to be. In the end, one would have no choice, it seems, but to concede that, if changes are to be possible, then the basic stuff must be entirely quality-free,[4] and this is merely to create a fresh problem, not to offer an explanation, for the immediate question is, what constitutes the identity of such a stuff as a subject of change?

So nothing really has been gained. The main theoretical motive behind the naturalistic theory of universal substance, as we saw, was the need to find a solution to the puzzle of existential change. The phenomenal world is full of perishable objects, and, given that coming into being or going out of existence cannot be attributes of any such objects, it seemed

---

[4] This, I take it, was the thought behind Anaximander's apeiron hypothesis.

that the only rational option was to interpret existential changes as modifications of an underlying and enduring universal substratum. However, as has been shown, such a universal substratum would of necessity have to remain indeterminate and indeterminable, and as such could not satisfy the logical requirements needed for it to perform the role of an identical subject of change. The theory thus provides no real insight either into what actually changes, or how changes come about, and is philosophically deeply flawed.[5]

Change and Naturalistic Pluralist Theories

A different but equally defective reductivist treatment of the phenomenal existential change is exemplified by the various versions of ontological atomism. The central idea here is that the basic material of which the phenomenal world is made up consists of a plurality of certain simple elements or entities, and that all change, in the final analysis, is due to the displacements and rearrangements of such entities, which themselves are impervious to any kind of (qualitative) alteration.[6] Instead of a single, enduring, universal substance, we now have a constellation of enduring simple substances.[7] But the disadvantage of this solution is that it paints a mechanistic, and hence much too simplistic and inadequate picture of change. There is no clue to how or why such simple substances form phenomenally identifiable clusters, or how they can produce the many-faceted world of our experience. If they are conceived as bare particulars,

[5] Some idealist philosophers, like Hegel for example, tried to remedy these difficulties by replacing the universal substance with a universal subject, and by interpreting change as a process whereby such a subject attains self-fulfilment.

[6] The 'right name for coming into being', says Anaxagoras, 'would be "being compounded", and for perishing "being dissolved"' (frag. 17).

[7] In some more recent atomistic theories (e.g. Russell's Logical Atomism) the emphasis has been on *logical* simplicity while permanence has been regarded as being of lesser importance. In fact, the tendency (among phenomenalists, in particular) has often been to say that the basic constituents of the world are inherently perishable and transient. However, despite this, such theories generally fail to address the problem of existential change and I am here concerned with those which do.

they almost by definition remain cognitively inaccessible and mysterious. (I should emphasize that my criticism here is directed against the naturalistic pluralist theories. Whilst I am prepared to concede that a form of pluralism is essential to change, I certainly do not believe that naturalistic pluralism is the right approach. See Chapter 6.)

Plato's alternative pluralist solution was to say that the basic entities, and the ultimate subjects of predication, were in fact certain characters or universals. This made it possible for him to take on board a much broader array of ontological objects, and, paradoxically, to produce a theory which—on the face of it, at least—did better justice to the complexity of the truth claims that we make about the world than any of the atomistic theories, given their extreme reductivist policies, were able to do. Nevertheless, the issue of change, not surprisingly, remained as intractable as before. More so, in fact; and it is clear why. It is one thing to be a genuine, or even fundamental, subject of predication, and quite another to be capable of acting as a subject of change, and in the case of characters the latter possibility is excluded almost by definition. Admittedly, collo-quially, and in an imprecise sort of way, we do ascribe change to characters. We say 'The colour of that garment has faded', 'The temperature in the room has fallen', etc. But such and similar locutions are merely convenient *ad hoc* devices conveying information that no one has any difficulty in recognizing as being essentially about changes in certain individuals. It is the garment that has faded—it is a lighter shade of its former colour—and it is the room that has grown colder. Plato was not saying anything out of the ordinary when he insisted on the immutability of characters. Characters are not corruptible. Moreover, the very idea that a character, or 'form', might be subject to change is incoherent, for if it did change in any genuine sense, it would cease to be the character it is. Least of all it can be said of a character that it can come into existence or cease to be. The only trouble was that having decided that characters were basic existents, Plato was left with no choice but to consign all change to the world of shadows.

The Dead-End of Naturalistic Ontology

This, of course, was a virtual admission of failure, not a solution. For changes, shadowy or otherwise, we certainly do experience, and the conceptual embarrassment that this presents is not likely to go away. Nevertheless, the failure of Plato's theory to deal satisfactorily with the problem is instructive, in that it helps to highlight the limitations of the frame of reference within which the problem of change is discussed in naturalistic ontology generally. The central task is seen as being one of identifying the basic subject, or subjects, of predication; and the problem of change is regarded, accordingly, as being one of determining which, if any, of such subjects of predication also qualify as subjects of change; or, to put the matter the other way round, whether there are any genuine subjects of change that can also properly be described as basic subjects of predication—the basic subjects of predication usually being treated as identical with basic existents. But on naturalistic premises this approach almost invariably leads to a denial of change at the fundamental level. The point is that change *qua* acquisition of contradictory predicates over time presupposes the capacity on the part of the subject of altering its attributes— or qualities—without becoming numerically different. We need the distinction, that is, between numerical identity and qualitative difference, and, conversely, between numerical difference and qualitative sameness. And, as was shown by our discussion of universal substance, on naturalistic premises no clear account can be given of such distinctions. There is precious little sense that in a naturalistic context can be extracted from the notion of a purely numerically enduring substratum of predication.[8] Plato was probably the first to appreciate fully the implications of this difficulty. He accepted that the basic subjects of predication could not endure numerically without enduring qualitatively, but a consequence of this, of course, was that—as long as one remained within the ambit of naturalistic ontology—at the fundamental level there could be

[8] In ch. 5 I shall discuss an attempt to solve this problem of traditional metaphysics in the context of a theory of universal development.

no change at all. (I shall revert to the topic of numerical and qualitative identity in Chapters 6 and 7.)[9]

Events and Change

In point of fact, as we shall see presently, one is bound to reach the same conclusion irrespective of whether things or events are taken as basic; which shows that the difficulties arising from the concept of change demand not a choice of different ontological items but a reconsideration of the manner in which ontological questions are asked.

[9] Aristotle's efforts, in opposition to Plato, to restore the position of empirical, and perishable, particulars as the basic subjects of predication, although broadly on the right lines, fell well short of providing a solution to the problem of change, mainly because no clarification was provided of the distinction between numerical and qualitative identity. Platonic forms re-emerge in Aristotle's ontology as 'formal causes' (Cf. *Metaph.* 983ᵃ), with the formal cause, in respect of its ontological status, being characterized by Aristotle as τὸ τί ἦν εἶναι (*quod erat esse*). This celebrated phrase has been the subject of much controversy among Aristotelian scholars, and some commentators have remarked on its suspect grammar as well as its philosophical mysteriousness (cf. J. Owens, *The Doctrine of Being in the Aristotelian Metaphysics*, 3rd edn. (Toronto, 1978), 173 ff.). In point of fact, this phrase, despite its grammatical 'oddity', is not nearly as mysterious as it is made out to be, and, it seems to me, points quite clearly to what is a central feature of platonic archetypes. It can be rendered in English reasonably naturally as 'that which was [always] to be'. The intention, in short, is to convey that formal causes, like platonic archetypes, are there, have been there, will be there, for all time. As regards empirical particulars, Aristotle's position is that they represent a unity of form (viz. the formal cause, in the sense just defined) and formless matter. But the problem is that this does not really help to explain how such hybrids of form and matter are capable of suffering change without changing their identity. Nor does it throw any light on what is involved in their coming into being or disappearing from existence. For what exactly is the existential change being predicated of in such a case? Formless matter by definition cannot exist on its own (and hence presumably cannot act as a genuine subject of predication anyway), whereas 'that which was [always] to be' is imperishable and unchanging. Empirical particulars are supposed to result from a fusion of these two elements; but how this can give us something of which it can be meaningfully said that it comes into and goes out of existence remains obscure. Aristotle himself seems to vacillate in his views regarding particular forms. Sometimes he says they are destructible (*Metaph.*, bk. 11, 1060ᵃ); at other times, he seems to suggest that strictly they are neither generated nor do they perish, but are just there at one time and not at another (ibid., bk. 7, 1039ᵇ). Cf. A. C. Lloyd, *Form and Universal in Aristotle* (Liverpool, 1981).

With regard to events, I said earlier that there are circumstances in which events as well as things can be significantly described as changing. A speech, a committee meeting, a concert performance, while still in progress, can change its character or direction in a variety of ways. But this means that, unless it can be shown that such changes can be interpreted in terms of changes of attributes of the entities involved in the events concerned, then we shall have no choice but to apply to events the categorial machinery of objects and attributes in much the same way as we do with things; and, if so, we are likely to encounter the same difficulties, and end up by being forced to concede that, fundamentally at any rate, changes do not take place at all.

If, on the other hand, we start with the assumption that events as such do not change, then we are going to find ourselves in an even greater quandary; for if events don't change, then, on the assumption that they are basic, evidently nothing does.

So how, if at all, is change possible? How can it be made intelligible? There is only one way, it seems, in which change might take place where events are concerned, and that is through events acquiring successively certain attributes that are such as leave their internal constitution intact, for example by altering their position in a time series. If this can be shown to be possible, then, it seems, the problem of change might be capable of being solved after all.

That there can be *no* such solution can be seen by considering McTaggart's celebrated proof of the unreality of time.[10] McTaggart's proof can be summarized as follows:

There are two ways of designating temporal order. One way is to say of an event that it happens earlier, at the same time as, or later than, some other event. The other is to say of an event that it occurs in the present, or that it occurred in the past, or that it lies in the future. The temporal determinations past, present, future represent what McTaggart calls the *A* series; whereas the series of positions in time that run from earlier to later is dubbed by him the *B* series. The temporal ordering via

[10] J. E. McTaggart, 'The Unreality of Time', *Mind*, 17 (Oct. 1908), 457–74.

earlier/later conveys certain permanent relations between events, in the sense that if an event N is earlier than an event M, then it is always true that N is earlier than M; and, conversely, it is always true that M is later than N. By contrast, an event can alter its position in the A series. Thus an event happening in the present was once future and will be past. The Allied invasion of Sicily during the Second World War took place before the invasion of Normandy, and after the Battle of Alamein, and the relations before and after are here fixed and permanent. But with regard to the A series, the invasion of Sicily was future at one time, then it became present, then past.

. Now superficially it might seem that the series running from earlier to later (the B series) as well as being more objective, or perhaps because of it, represents a more fundamental feature of time compared with the indexical distinctions of the A series, which issue from whenever 'present' happens to be. This is denied on the grounds that, although events must be capable of being members of the B series as well as the A series, it is only through the A-series distinctions that time can be grasped at all. Time involves change, and in the B series, strictly, nothing changes. Events occupy always the same position in the series and never alter any of their features. Moreover, they are individuated by their location in the series. If an event ever did change its serial position, it would cease to be numerically the same event. But it can neither begin nor cease to be the same event. In other words, there can be no change; and if there is no change, there is no time.

The only possibility, then, of change occurring is via the A series. Yet the A series, according to McTaggart, involves a contradiction, and hence cannot exist. Past, present, and future, he argues, are incompatible characteristics: while every event must be ascribable to at least one of them, it cannot be coherently ascribed more than one. Nevertheless, every event has all three. If an event is past, it was present and future; if it is present, it was future and will be past; if it is future, it will be present and past. But if every event has all three characteristics, then evidently there cannot be either time or change.

Now the immediate objection to this might be that 'is present', 'was future', 'will be past' are themselves not in-

compatible predicates for they ascribe to events the characteristics in question in different temporal modes. However, it is
easily seen that this objection involves an infinite regress; for
by ascribing temporal predicates to events in different temporal
modes, as above, one is merely making use of the distinctions
of tense, as applicable to events, in order to show how events
can have different temporal predicates. What one is saying, in
effect, is that an event is present in the present, future in the
past, and past in the future; so that nothing really has been
gained, for we are confronted with exactly the same problem as
before.

In short, the *A* series cannot be applied to reality without
producing a contradiction. But, then, it cannot be valid of
reality; and since time stands and falls with the *A* series, time is
unreal; and so is change.

Phenomenological and Objective Time

The above conclusion is false, of course, for what the argument
shows is not that time, and hence change too, are illusory, but
merely that past, present, and future are not properties of
naturalistically conceived events.

However, before I consider this in more detail, it is necessary
to set to rest any lingering impression that the alleged
contradiction might be obviated if things rather than events
were taken as basic items, on the grounds that the capacity of
successively acquiring incompatible attributes is implicit in the
very concept of a thing. I have already discussed earlier some
fundamental difficulties involved in trying to explain change in
terms of things. All that it is necessary to point out at this stage
is that the idea of a successive acquisition of incompatible
attributes already presupposes time, and hence (in terms of the
argument) it presupposes the applicability of the *A* series; and
so the contradiction will not have been avoided. The point, in
short, is that we would find ourselves in the position of having
to ascribe all three incompatible *A*-series characteristics to

things and their properties, whereas before we were ascribing them to events.[11]

Returning now to the above argument, its main weakness stems from its underlying assumption that time and change can be accepted as 'real' only on condition that the *A*-series predicates can be shown to be true of events independently of our beliefs about events. But quite clearly any attempt to show this must result in absurdities. Past, present, and future are not properties of events, or any other ontological items for that matter. They are primarily modalities of experience: the manner in which events present themselves to us in acts of perception, recollection, or anticipation.

If they are properties of events, in what way exactly do they qualify events? How long does the 'present' event last? It lasts as long as the event itself. 'Presentness' does not signify any determinate, objective duration. As McTaggart himself appreciates,[12] it is sufficient to raise such questions to realize that nothing much is to be gained by pursuing this route. 'Presentness' is a phenomenological concept. There is no clock for measuring 'objective' present. But then what might a statement to the effect that an event 'occurs in the present', or 'is present', be said to convey? If any meaning can be attached to it at all, then it is only as a report of the experience of 'presentness', or the experience of something being *given* in the present (as distinct from the experience of something being recollected in memory, or anticipated).

Which does not, I hasten to add, make the *A*-series characteristics entirely subjective. The subjective aspect of temporal distinctions is unquestionably of central importance. There is nothing that can be intelligibly said about time unless 'present' can be connected with the experienced, or phenomenological, present. What is more, no two phenomenological presents need necessarily be of the same duration. What is present for me need not be present for you, and vice versa. Nevertheless, as I

---

[11] That McTaggart's argument works just as well with objects (or 'things', in the sense in which I am here using the latter term) as it does with events was shown by M. Dummett. See his paper 'A Defence of McTaggart's Proof of the Unreality of Time', in *Truth and Other Enigmas* (London, 1978), 351–8.

[12] Cf. ibid. 472 f.

shall argue later on, it is incoherent to assume that this could always be the case—that my own phenomenological time could be permanently out of phase with any other phenomenological time. We share in an intersubjective time which we call history. Phenomenological diachrony between experienced times by different subjects of experiences is a frequent occurrence, but it is not, nor can it be, a universal phenomenon.

If this is accepted, then the paradox allegedly generated by the *A* series can be seen to evaporate. The false assumption underlying the above argument is that the reality of time depends on the possibility of ascribing 'now' to some specific ontological items, and of course there are no such items. The so-called *A* series represents the temporal distinctions based on the experienced now. It is what might be called a schematic expansion of the phenomenological time. But being anchored in experienced time does not make the *A* series any less real, if only because the *A* series can be shared.

Here then we have our answer. The *A* series is based on certain temporal modes of experiencing. At the same time, through its intersubjective aspects, it enables us to extend our temporal concepts to encompass the *B*-series positions that run from earlier to later. The two series are not in conflict with each other; rather they are structurally interlinked, the key link between them being the intersubjectively shared present. I shall revert to the topic of objectivity in Chapter 6.

The Necessity of Tense

It follows from the above that the fundamental facts about time and change cannot be expressed without a tensed language, that is, a language in which the relevant inflexions of 'to be' are understood with reference to a phenomenological 'now'. Yet the naturalistic impulse, which usually disguises itself as common sense, has often inspired arguments designed to show the logical dispensability of tense. Consider one such argument.[13]

[13] The argument presented below is D. H. Mellor's (*Real Time*). All the comments in the present section refer to the views advanced by Mellor in this book.

Descriptions of events involving tensed verbs, it is argued, do not convey any tensed facts. There are no such facts. The world is intrinsically tenseless. This does not mean that time is unreal. McTaggart inferred from the contradictions he detected in the tensed view of time that neither time nor change really existed. But this was a false inference. What is unreal, if anything, is tense not time. Real time represents a series of positions characterized by the relation of earlier/later and suitably conveyed with the help of dates. When an event is dated, it is placed within an objective framework within which tense plays no role. Admittedly we normally employ verbal tense when attributing dates. Thus we might say 'The French Revolution occurred in 1789', indicating that it happened in the past. But the objective content of such a statement, that is, the content relevant to its truth or falsehood, could equally well be expressed in terms of tenseless present, by saying 'The French Revolution occurs (tenselessly) in 1789.'

This immediately prompts several questions: (1) If there are no tensed facts, what do tensed statements really mean? What exactly is their objective content? (2) Why are such statements necessary? What purpose do they serve? Why cannot they be dispensed with altogether? (3) If, as is claimed, real time is tenseless, then it should be possible to provide a tenseless account of the experience of the passage of time. But how can this be achieved? I shall argue that such answers as are provided to such questions by the theory here under discussion are all unsatisfactory, and do not add to our understanding of the problem of change. Change, I shall argue, requires an appeal to tense.

With regard to (1), it is claimed that the meaning of tensed statements is given by their truth conditions, and that such conditions can be stated in tenseless terms. Consider the following example. I might say 'I began reading this book an hour ago'. The peculiar feature of this statement is that it contains an implicit reference to its own utterance, that is, it is 'token reflexive'. An inevitable consequence of this is that the objective (clock) time of its utterance will have to be taken into account in any consideration of its truth or falsehood. Similarly, 'this book' will not be any old book but the one that lies open in front of me at the time I make my statement. It follows that it is possible to state the truth conditions of what is being said without employing either demonstratives or tense. Thus the statement will be true provided exactly an hour separates the time when I (tenselessly) begin to read the book in hard, green covers in front of me from the time when I (tenselessly) utter my statement.

In short, the thesis is that tense in the final analysis makes no difference to truth. The conditions that need to be satisfied for tensed statements to be true can all be expressed in a tense-free form. Moreover, tensed statements differ in respect of their logically relevant meaning only to the extent to which they differ in respect of their truth conditions. This does not mean, so the argument goes, that tensed statements can be simply translated into, and replaced by, tenseless ones, for what puts tensed statements into a separate category is precisely the circumstance that their truth conditions depend upon the time of their utterance.

But this explanation is clearly unsatisfactory. It is claimed that the meaning of tensed statements is given by their truth conditions (which themselves can be stated without making use of tense), and, moreover, that the reason why tensed statements cannot be translated into tenseless ones is due to the specificity of their truth conditions. But the key question, of course, is why there should be a difference in truth conditions between tensed and tenseless statements, and, in particular, how do we understand such a difference? It is not enough to say that the difference arises because of the relevance that the time of utterance has to truth. What needs to be explained is just why the time of utterance has an effect on truth, and this can hardly be done without referring to the indexical properties of tense; in other words, it is necessary to understand tense before we can understand why tensed statements have the truth conditions they do. It is their specific meaning that determines their truth conditions, rather than their truth conditions determining their meaning. To argue that tense makes no difference to truth is just an expression of a naturalistic bias.

Consider now (2): Why are tensed statements necessary? The answer given to this is that we need such statements not in

order to express any tensed facts, but in order to express our
beliefs, which in turn help to explain our actions. Thus if I want
to hear the one o'clock news, my belief that one o'clock is now
will cause me to switch on the radio.

But this will not do either, for beliefs too are facts, albeit facts
of a special sort. Consider the following state of affairs. Given
my feeling of lassitude, although I happen to believe it is now
one o'clock, this won't make me get out of my chair and switch
on the radio, much as I would like to hear the news. This piece
of reporting includes a statement about my belief, and in so far
as tense necessarily enters into a description of such a belief,
clearly there is no justification in claiming that all the facts
about time can be expressed without ever making use of tense;
and hence that tense has no 'basis in reality'.[14]

Which brings us to (3). If the aim is to show that there are no
tensed facts, it is necessary to show, as a minimum condition,
that a tenseless account can be provided of the phenomenological
or indexical time. The theory under discussion pursues this aim
by attempting to explain the perception of a temporal order in
terms of what is termed a 'causal' order. The direction of time, it
is claimed, is the direction of causation. The argument put
forward is essentially as follows. The perception of a temporal
order presupposes temporally ordered perceptions. To perceive
an event A preceding an event B is to perceive A first, then B,
with the perception of B including a recollection or some
memory trace of the perception of A. But this points to the
existence of a causal relation between the perceptions concerned.
My perceptions are experienced as temporally ordered because
they are causally ordered. It is because my perception of A
objectively precedes my perception of B that I see A preceding
B, rather than the other way round.

The idea, in short, is that my experience of temporal order is
based on, and presupposes, an objective order, and since
objective order can be described in tenseless terms, tense is not

---

[14] I quote an amusing *non sequitur* from Mellor's book: 'Although tense is not
an aspect of reality, to us who act in time it is an inescapable mode of
perceiving, thinking and speaking about reality' (p. 6). Since he presumably
accepts that 'those who act in time' are also part of reality, tensed thoughts
surely can hardly fail to represent certain 'aspects of reality'. Or does he perhaps
have some other reasons for disbelieving this inference?

a feature of objective reality, and is irrelevant to real time. But the argument fails to prove anything of the sort, for it can easily be stood on its head and turned against itself. Thus one could just as well argue that perceptions are 'objectively' ordered as they are because they are thus given in our experience and not otherwise. The point is that there is no way of determining the objective order of perceptions *independently* of the perceived order. But, if not, then no appeal to causal relation will enable us to get rid of tense.

Take, for example, my current experience of listening to music. That certain features of this experience follow certain other features in a temporal sequence is part of its pheno-menological structure. It is how this experience is apperceived in reflective consciousness. It clearly does not make sense to speak of its temporal direction being determined by the 'causal' relation between its earlier and subsequent phases, for we have to presuppose an understanding of 'earlier' and 'subsequent' before we can even begin to explain what is involved in the causal relation in question.

The clue to temporal order, in short, must be sought within experiences themselves; or, more accurately, in the form in which experiences occur within the framework of the experienced time. The distinctions of tense are not intelligible independently of experienced time, and experienced time is a biographically structured time. Past, present, and future are part of the structure of a unitary biographical sequence. The unity of such a sequence is a fundamental phenomenological datum and the necessary precondition of an understanding of any temporal order.

Tense, Change, and Teleology

The point is, if there is no observer-related time, there is no time. The naturalistic impulse that inspires attempts to prove that a logically adequate description of reality can dispense with tense merely leaves us exposed to the ravages of scepticism, for once tense is abandoned, it is no longer possible to ward off the sceptical assault on the reality of time. And if the reality of time is called into question, so inevitably is the reality of change.

I am not suggesting, of course, that we do not convey facts about time and change without employing tense. We indicate time and change with the help of clock and calendar. But this way of talking about time and change conveys temporal distinctions only against the background of the distinctions of tense. There is nothing intrinsically temporal about the order of dates. Such an order acquires temporal significance only in relation to our ability to distinguish between before and after in respect of an experienced now.

McTaggart rightly regarded the distinction of past, present, and future as fundamental to an understanding of both time and change. But in an attempt to disprove the reality of time he made it easy for himself by assuming, in effect, that the supposition that time is real depended on the possibility of treating such determinations as properties of certain ontological items. He was then triumphantly able to show that any attempt to treat them that way immediately generated contradictions, since if any such item possessed any one of these 'properties', it inevitably possessed all three. But, of course, what this showed, if anything, was not that time and change were unreal but simply that no coherent account of time and change could be provided if the world was conceived of as an assemblage of certain ontological items (things, events, or whatever) and their properties. In a sense, McTaggart's argument against time, like Zeno's arguments against change, can be seen as an attempt at a *reductio ad absurdum* of naturalism.

But perhaps there is still an escape route available to the naturalist metaphysician, provided he is willing to show a degree of flexibility in his approach. Thus it might seem, superficially at any rate, that a judicious use of teleological concepts might enable him to give an account of change that would stand up better to the sceptical challenge. Let us now explore this possibility.

4

CHANGES AND ENDS

THE collapse of the 'causal' model, as we saw, seemed to indicate that there was no possibility of explaining why any two events, or states, should be mutually connected other than in the context of our experience; and this in turn raised the problem of accounting for change as an objective phenomenon. But surely, it might be said, such difficulties were due entirely to the exaggerated emphasis being placed upon efficient or mechanistic causation, exemplified by the proverbial billiard balls bouncing randomly off each other. Small wonder that under such circumstances the task of explaining the structure of the transition from A to B became an insurmountable problem. Any attempt to account for change in terms of mechanistic causation is a forlorn effort, destined to end in failure. Once this became obvious, the tendency, not unnaturally, was to retreat into the 'ontologically uncommitted' language of sufficient conditions. Now, within limits this may have been a sound practical policy, but from a philosophical point of view it was unsatisfactory, inasmuch as it meant in effect turning one's back on the problem of change rather than solving it.

What is required, if progress is to be made at all, so the argument might be continued, is a radical change of course, involving a reinterpretation of causation in terms of final causation. If events are treated not just as fortuitous (or fortuitously regular) successor events of previous happenings but rather as the latter's target states, then surely the Zenonian–Humean type of hurdle to an understanding of the possibility of change can be easily overcome, for in that case there is no longer any question of events being logically independent of each other. Every event *qua* target state necessarily presupposes the existence of certain antecedent source states, which in turn are themselves target states of yet earlier events, and so on. In a teleological context there are no fortuitous or logically isolated happenings. The phenomenon of change, within such a context, can thus be made perfectly intelligible in terms of accomplishment of certain ends.

This, prima facie, looks like a more promising line of approach, and, in what follows, I propose to explore it in more detail, in order to see if it can be supported with sufficiently cogent arguments and defended from criticism.

The 'Naturalness' of Purposes

In general, the purposive account of phenomena is closer to our natural ways of thinking, and it is only in modern times—in the aftermath of the intellectual upheaval that we associate with the birth of Renaissance science, to be precise—that the causal explanation in the narrow sense, based, that is, on a notion of causality emptied of all suggestion of purposiveness, gained prevalence. Yet the temptation to use a teleological language, even in a scientific context, remains strong, and it is not unusual to see those who deprecate the use of such a language as a matter of general principle succumb to its allure in practice.[1] This natural impulse, it seems to me, points generally in the right direction, and indicates what is substantially the correct view, namely, that a satisfactory account of the conditions that make changes possible, if such an account is to be possible at all, can be provided only from a teleological point of view.

Nevertheless, we shall have to guard against naturalistic distortions; and to this end it will be necessary to keep the distinction between human and natural teleology clearly in mind. In a human context, purposive behaviour is usually associated with voluntary action. But we also use the concept of purposiveness in a wider sense, to embrace all kinds of directively organized but non-voluntary behaviour. As Aristotle already pointed out, purpose, or, in his definition, 'that for the sake of which something comes about', does not necessarily

---

[1] In a recent TV lecture on the planets I heard a well-known astronomer say: 'The planet Mercury moves faster than the other planets in order not to fall on the Sun.' This account of the matter would have pleased the Greeks.

require a deliberating agent.[2] The issue is highly important, precisely because there is a tendency among those who accept the general principles of teleological explanation but try to underplay the aspect of voluntariness in purposive behaviour to assimilate the teleological explanation to the naturalistic stance. I shall argue that this is an error, and in particular that it is futile to try to construct a more plausible naturalist account of change by importing teleological categories into the framework of a naturalistic ontology. Any such attempt is misconceived and leads to nothing.

However, we must consider first some anti-teleological arguments.

The Teleology of Change and Scientific Explanation

There are two kinds of opposition to regarding goals and purposes as legitimate instruments of explanation: one limited and selective, the other unconditional. Those who take the moderate line are on the whole willing to concede that an appeal to goals and purposes, while inappropriate in some domains, is heuristically useful and indeed unavoidable in others. Thus whereas teleological concepts are out of place in natural sciences like physics or chemistry, they have an important role to play in such disciplines as history, sociology, and psychology. By contrast, those who take the hard line argue that any appeal to goals and purposes is, at best, an inferior expedient where a more accurate and comprehensive non-teleological account of phenomena is as yet unavailable, and, at worst is positively misleading and harmful. Explanatory models that depend on a consideration of goals and purposes, they argue, strictly fall outside science proper.

There are difficulties with both these views. The main problem for those who take the moderate approach is one of deciding exactly where a reference to goals and purposes is, and where it is not, appropriate. One obvious area of disagreement

---

[2] Cf. *Ph.*, bk. 2, 199[b].

is biology. According to the traditional Aristotelian view—of which 'vitalism' is the most radical modern version—every organism has its own entelechy, that is, its own inherent final cause which governs its development and generally makes it function as it does. But the idea of such entelechies is just as vigorously repudiated by others, including those who are not averse to accepting some form of teleological explanation, even in biology, let alone in disciplines that are concerned with typically human behaviour. Clearly if goals and purposes are to be admitted as valid instruments of explanation, the question that needs to be answered is, what goals and what purposes, and in what contexts?

With regard to the radical anti-teleological approach, on the other hand, the main difficulty confronting those who espouse it is one of devising a logically adequate non-teleological account of the vast array of phenomena that we normally describe in teleological terms. It is argued that teleology is incompatible with the principles of experimentally based rigorous science. Scientific disciplines, it is emphasized, do not divide into two categories: those which do and those which don't allow goals and purposes into their explanations. Science does not speak with two different tongues. However, the problem with this view is one of showing that all types of explanation do indeed fit into the same theoretical mould. To put it differently, what is needed is a proof that all ostensibly purposive events and activities can be described in non-teleological terms without any loss of truth, and it is hard to see how such a proof can be forthcoming.

I should point out that my principal concern here is not to try to settle the dispute concerning the putative division within science but to clarify the conditions of the possibility of change. Nevertheless, since part of the thesis that I am advancing is that change depends for its intelligibility on teleological concepts, it will be necessary to enter into a more detailed discussion of the view that such concepts are eliminable from a scientific description of the world, or, at least, that explanatory accounts in which they occur can be rephrased in such a way that they become compatible with the principles of experimental science.

Purposes and Functions

Let us begin, first, by considering some attempts to do the latter, in particular by translating what is regarded as the mystery-laden idiom of 'goals' and 'purposes' into the more down-to-earth language of 'functions'. Consider a rather banal example. The main purpose of the salivary glands is to facilitate ingestion of food by producing mucous fluid, which moistens it and softens it in the mouth. But surely, it might be said, all this can be expressed more simply as well as more accurately without talking of purposes, for example, by saying that production of mucous fluid which facilitates the ingestion of food is the function that the salivary glands as a matter of fact perform within the context of the normal life of the organism. Or take another example. It is the function of the lungs in mammals to aerate the blood. But to say this is merely to say that that is what the lungs actually do, no more and no less. The body, through blood, absorbs oxygen and expels carbon dioxide produced by food combustion. This process takes place in the lungs. It does not have to take place in the lungs. It is conceivable that the body could absorb oxygen and get rid of the carbon dioxide in some other way. As is well known, the heart-and-lung machine can perform the same function (hence the name). To say that the lungs have the function they do is merely to report an accident of evolution.

The teleological explanation can thus be stripped of its mysterious features, and reduced to something quite ordinary and empirically respectable. For all that is now being talked about is the kind of work that the salivary glands or the lungs as a matter of fact do in a particular context, and that is a testable proposition.

The functionalist interpretation of purposiveness along the lines sketched out above, it seems, brings at least two immediate advantages, both of considerable consequence. First, it seems effectively to forestall any slide from the talk of goals and purposes into the metaphysics of final causes, which—according to the popular view—bedevilled ancient science and was the chief obstacle to scientific progress until the

Galilean revolution finally liberated natural science from its shackles. The purpose that a given object may happen to fulfil in a given case is now seen simply as its accidental contextual function, not its entelechy. Admittedly, with regard to human artefacts in particular, the object in question may be deliberately designed to serve a particular purpose. Nevertheless, whilst the structure of its design may restrict the range of its possible use, the purpose embodied in its design does not necessarily determine the actual use to which that object may be put on a particular occasion. Moreover, and quite apart from this, the institutionalized function that a given object performs, or comes to acquire, within a given social context may and often does change, as social customs and practices change and develop. The mace was once a weapon of war, but now it serves merely as a symbol of authority vested in a collective body (for example, Parliament).

A second advantage of the functionalist account seems to be that it makes it possible to bring the biological and the mechanical systems, so to speak, under the same theoretical roof. Thus the kind of description that was given of the role of salivary glands, or of the lungs, can equally be given of mechanical devices like thermostats. The salivary glands produce a mucous fluid which as a matter of fact facilitates ingestion of food. Similarly, the thermostat operates as a circuit breaker which as a matter of fact helps keep the temperature at the required level. It is not an intrinsic purpose of the thermostat to regulate temperature; it is simply the work that it happens to perform within the particular kind of mechanical set-up. Of course the thermostat was specifically designed to perform this role. But the link between its intended purpose and its actual function in any given situation is not a necessary one. An artefact intended by its designer for a specific purpose may end up performing a variety of different functions which have nothing to do with its original assignation. If I use my spectacle lenses to focus the sun's rays on to a piece of paper in order to set it on fire, I am using them for a purpose for which they were not intended. Nevertheless, their function in the context of the operation in hand is quite specific and well defined. And, of course, it is possible that in different contexts they might be put to any number of other uses. It follows that there is no need to appeal to any intended, let alone inherent, goals or purposes to explain the role that an object performs on a given occasion. A functional description suffices. This is as true of organic structures as it is of mechanical devices. But, then, there is no question of there being any irreparable theoretical cleavage within science, as some falsely assume there must be. Science is one and indivisible.

Criticism of the Functional Account

How justified are these claims? The obvious difficulty is how to account for the voluntary activity of the agent. If the functionalist interpretation is going to work, it must be possible to give an adequate description of voluntary action in functional terms, and it is not clear how this can be achieved. Consider the following example. Suppose that while walking in the street I see some distance away an acquaintance heading in my direction, and, being rather anxious to avoid him, hurriedly cross over to the other side. Then my crossing of the road fulfils the function of enabling me to avoid the person concerned only in the light of my *intention* to avoid him. If there is no intention, there is no function.

But let us leave the problem of voluntary action to one side for the time being, and pursue the matter of non-voluntary purposive behaviour, which may appear easier to deal with from a functionalist standpoint. What is being suggested is (1) that a functional paraphrase of a teleological explanation can in effect dispense with the notion of a goal; and (2) that functions in general represent accidental rather than essential properties of 'teleologically' behaving objects. Take again the example of salivary glands. It is argued that the teleological explanation 'The salivary glands produce mucous fluid *in order* to facilitate ingestion of food by moistening it in the mouth' can be reproduced without 'in order to', or any such similar expressions, with all its truth-relevant content remaining intact. A 'functional' account is said merely to report the kind of activity that actually goes on in a given case, allowing the possibility that the object in question might in principle perform any number of different functions in different contexts. As it happens, the salivary glands, in addition to their main function, already perform a digestive role in a small way. But, quite apart from this, there is no reason (this is the implication) why it should not be possible to transplant them, say, to another part of the body, where they would play an entirely different role that may, nevertheless, be compatible with their internal structure.

By contrast, from the orthodox teleological point of view, the fact that the salivary glands facilitate ingestion of food by producing mucous fluid is part of their essential description. The salivary glands would not be what they are if they did not perform this role. Similarly for the lungs. Teleologically, in short, the emphasis is not just on what they as a matter of fact do, but on what they have to do in order to serve the purpose they actually serve within the relevant organic context. Their purpose within that context is part of their definition.

In fact, it is possible to take the teleological argument a stage further, by pointing out, for example, that often it is the concrete context of which such an organ forms part, not merely the type of context, that matters. If this were not so, the problem of tissue rejection in organ transplants would never arise. That it does arise, it might be argued, shows that an adequate account of the function of bodily organs cannot be given without making use of teleological concepts. For the built-in genetic design in the tissue of such organs is tuned in with the design of the organism as a whole; with the result that it can successfully perform its function only within the specific genetic environment which it helps to sustain. It derives its purpose from the system of which it is a constituent. It is, so to speak, custom-made for the system. All of which seems to show that the concept of a goal—goal *qua* object or *qua* target state—cannot be entirely written out of a description of what actually takes place on any given occasion. An account in terms of 'accidental' functions, without any reference to goals, may be possible for thermostats, but it does not work with living organisms.

Target States and the Negative-Feedback Model

The central issue thus seems to be whether purposes, involving references to certain target states, can, at least in some cases, be treated as part of the essential properties of 'teleologically' behaving objects, or whether they all can be naturalistically interpreted as reducing to accidental functions of such objects. As is clear from my remarks so far, I am taking the former view. Moreover, I shall argue that, unless it is possible to treat purposes as essential properties, there is no hope of providing a rational account of the possibility of change.

However, there are some more sophisticated naturalistic interpretations of teleology that we shall have to look at first. I begin with a subtler and more elaborate version of the functional theory of purposive behaviour, based on the so-called negative-feedback model. On the face of it, this model seems to offer the possibility of taking on board the concept of goal as well as providing the machinery for understanding the moves needed for achievement of goals, while at the same time precluding any interpretation of goals in terms of final causes.

Not all purposive behaviour, of course, demands the actual existence of the goal-object (or the focal object of the target state aimed at). My attempts to find a cure for baldness, or discover a tenth planet, or prove Fermat's last theorem are no less purposive for the fact that I may be engaged in a wild-goose chase. However, in the present context I am not specifically interested in defining the minimal conditions of purposive behaviour but in the relevance of purposes in general to an account of the conditions of the possibility of change.

Consider a bat chasing an insect. The bat emits high-frequency sound pulses which it receives back as echoes as they bounce off objects, and thereby regulates its flight to avoid obstacles and home in on its prey. The emitted signal returns as input information, which is rapidly processed, leading to adjustments in the overall energy output and the required flight corrections. The bat's flight path is thus governed by what is technically known as 'negative feedback', that is, the signal indicating such margin of error as separates the direction of the bat's flight path from the position of the target.

The vast array of machines from relatively simple servo-mechanisms like the photoelectric cells operating lift doors to complex industrial robots work on this principle, and, if 'purposiveness' can be defined in terms of negative feedback, then their behaviour too can be characterized as purposive. Some of the most spectacular examples of negative feedback are notoriously provided by some modern weaponry. A heat-seeking anti-aircraft missile picks up the emission of infra-red rays generated by the aircraft in flight and homes in on the area of their strongest source around the engine exhaust, as it pursues its target along the latter's uneven course, adjusting and altering its own flight path as it does so. In this, it behaves no differently from a bat trying to catch an insect, or a tiger pursuing an antelope. It is involved in a complex series of manœuvres, while trying to compensate for its quarry's evasive action. In all such cases a vast amount of information is received and processed by both the pursuer and the quarry, with the alterations of informational input resulting in the corresponding changes in performance output.

The negative-feedback model thus makes it possible to cope with situations that involve a flexible response to changed circumstances in the pursuit of a specific goal, but the basic strategy of interpreting purposes in terms of 'accidental' functions remains unchanged. Thus the purposive behaviour of the bat chasing an insect is explained in terms of the input/output schema, with the input signals eliciting—as a matter of fact rather than necessity—a 'goal-directed' action of a particular sort. Or, more accurately, the bat is in a specific functional state that, looked at externally, appears as an act of homing in on a particular insect. The point is that the bat's homing in on the insect is not part of the essential description of the bat's functional state. But then clearly it must be possible to account for its goal-directed behaviour without employing teleological terms at all.

Let us pursue this line of thought a little further. The bat chases the insect, correcting and modifying its flight path as it does so, guided by the sound-waves bouncing off its target. Since many moths are equipped with a defensive mechanism enabling them to pick up the bat's high-frequency sound pulses, they are able, even in complete darkness, to take avoiding action, including suddenly dropping to the ground, and escape. The signal that the bat receives is of variable intensity and it may even cease completely for a brief moment as the insect flies behind an obstacle, but the bat's guidance mechanism is able to cope with such variations of input signal, provided they do not exceed certain limits. A great deal will depend on the circumstances of the chase and the amount of information that needs to be processed while the chase is going on.

The bat's flight course at any given time is thus dependent on a number of specifiable parameters. These parameters may oscillate in value relative to each other, but, provided these oscillations are not excessive, the bat continues to pursue its quarry. Now it might be argued that on any given occasion the bat's goal-directed behaviour not only depends causally upon a number of specifiable parameters, but can in fact be defined in terms of those parameters.'And if this can be done, then we do not need to use teleological language to describe its behaviour.

Let us use the term 'G-state' to describe the bat's goal-directed, quarry-chasing behaviour in a given instance. Then whether, or for how long, the bat will remain in the G-state will depend on how hungry it is, on the strength and the continuity of the signal received from the quarry, on the amount of interference from other sources, weather conditions, etc. All these parameters may fluctuate in value, but, as we have just said, if such fluctuations are not too large, they are usually compensated for by suitable adjustments in behavioural response, and the bat stays on course. Thus the bat compensates for variations in wind resistance or alterations in air current by suitably modifying its flight path, or simply by increasing its energy output. In short, the bat's behaviour remains 'directively organized' as a result of a whole constellation of factors that are all causally interrelated. But then we don't need to use specifically teleological concepts to account for the bat's behaviour, for the bat's G-state can be defined in terms of the (causal) conditions for a directively organized system.[3]

The Negative-Feedback Model and the Idea of Compensation

The above argument is vitiated by its dependence upon the idea of compensation. It is claimed that the fact that the bat persists in a certain state that we ordinarily describe in teleological terms is causally determined by a number of concomitant factors. Not all of these factors have the same effect on the bat's behaviour, and, as the circumstances change, so their relative causal influence on the bat's behaviour changes too. But the key point is that the bat remains in a directively organized state by compensating for any oscillations in their value. It is the activity of compensation that characterizes its behaviour, although the point may be reached when compensation is no longer possible and the bat, as a result, leaves the G-state.

But the question is, just what is being compensated and why? How can the compensatory activity be explained as 'compensatory' without employing teleological language? Admittedly we often use the concept of compensation within a purely mechanical context. Thus in some computerized cars the malfunctioning of a part which in normal circumstances would immobilize the engine is automatically compensated for by certain modifications elsewhere in the system, usually at the cost of increased fuel consumption. But to describe what is taking place as an activity of compensation already presupposes familiarity with the notion of a target state.

Moreover, it seems that the notion of a target state is not only essential to an understanding of certain types of behaviour, but that it is a precondition of intelligibility of any process of change, in this sense: that in the final analysis it is only from the point of view of a target state that we can have an adequate grasp of what it is for a sequence of events to be part of a

[3] The above is a simplified version of an argument advanced by Ernest Nagel in 'Teleological Explanation', in J. V. Canfield (ed.), *Purpose in Nature* (Englewood Cliffs, NJ, 1966).

homogeneous and structured process of change rather than representing merely a series of fortuitous happenings that ontologically may not be linked with each other at all. I shall return to this later on.

Of course not all target states are attainable, and, as we saw earlier, many are impossible to attain. If I am unable to find a tenth planet, this may be due simply to the fact that there isn't one. But if I cannot square the circle, this is because the solution is logically impossible. Nevertheless, the idea of a target state remains unaffected by this.

The Reductivist Strategy and Accounts of Actions

The attempt to demonstrate the dispensability of all references to target states from a scientific description of the world echoes the similar attempt (discussed in Chapter 2) to eliminate the need to appeal to efficient causes. In both cases, the reductivist argument is inspired by the desire to avoid what are perceived as the unnecessary metaphysical entanglements associated with these concepts and to free science from what are considered to be untestable propositions. In any case, it is sometimes argued, it is pointless to dispute over whether the world *per se* is causally ordered or whether there are irreducibly teleological facts, if the scientifically relevant content in any given situation can be perfectly adequately expressed without employing either causal or teleological categories. Any causal or teleological explanation can be paraphrased into a set of inferentially linked propositions which do not feature either type of concept. Explanatory accounts of phenomena reduce to deductive arguments, whereby the explanandum, namely, the proposition reporting a given event, can be shown to follow from a general premiss, or 'covering law', under certain specified conditions, with both causal and teleological explanations essentially being expressible in terms of such deductive-nomological or 'covering-law' explanations.

With regard to causal explanations in particular, as we recall, the key concept in the reductivist paraphrase was that of sufficient conditions. Thus in saying of a person, for example,

that he caught typhoid fever because he drank water contaminated with *salmonella typhi* is—according to the reductivist
view—just another way of saying that, other things being
equal, the fact that that person ingested the bacterium is a
sufficient condition of his showing the symptoms characteristic
of the disease.

A similar treatment is accorded to teleological accounts of
non-voluntary behaviour. To take again the example of salivary
glands, the statement to the effect that the salivary glands
lubricate the area of the mouth and the alimentary tract 'in
order' to facilitate the ingestion of food is seen as a somewhat
fanciful representation of a state of affairs that can be expressed
more simply and accurately by saying that such glands as a
matter of fact facilitate ingestion of food in virtue of producing
the fluid that makes this possible; or, to put it differently, other
things being equal, the production of such a fluid is a sufficient
condition of unimpeded ingestion of food.

In short, in both types of case the modified explanation is
couched in terms of sufficient conditions, and there is no
mention of either causes or purposes.

But now consider actions. Can '*A* went to the greengrocer's to
buy some oranges' be analysed in a similar way to '*A* went
down with typhoid fever because he drank water infected with
the bacterium' or 'The salivary glands produce mucous fluid in
order to facilitate ingestion of food'? Given that greengrocers
sell oranges, it is of course reasonable that *A* should go to the
greengrocer's to make his purchase. But it would have been
equally reasonable for him to go to the local supermarket, or
anywhere else where oranges happen to be on sale. *A*'s desire to
buy oranges plus the fact that greengrocers sell oranges do not
by themselves add up to an explanation why *A* decided to go to
the greengrocer's in preference to some other place. What is
more, even if he had made it a habit to buy his fruit at the
greengrocer's, this would still not necessarily constitute a
sufficient ground for his going to the greengrocer's, for there are
any number of reasons why he may have chosen to break his
habit on that particular occasion.

It follows that it is not possible to recast '*A* went to the
greengrocer's to buy some oranges' as an inference, whereby

A's action could be explained as a logical consequence of some law-like proposition, or propositions, linking visits to green-grocers to the desire to buy oranges. And this suggests the conclusion that in the case of actions, at least, the strategy of hypothetico-deductive paraphrase fails to provide a means of obviating or dispensing with teleological concepts.

What is relevant in any consideration of reasons for action are of course the agent's own beliefs. Yet even beliefs become relevant factors only in the light of the agent's own intentions. A's desire to buy oranges evidently could not be accepted as a valid reason for his going to the greengrocer's if he did not believe that he was likely to find them there; but, although his belief makes his reason appropriate, it does not explain why he went to the greengrocer's rather than anywhere else.

The Necessity of Purposes

In fact, I wish to go further and argue that, appearances to the contrary, even in the case of non-voluntary behaviour, references to goals *qua* target states, in some form or another, are an indispensable ingredient of any comprehensive explanatory account of the events that are taking place.

The central issue here seems to be whether and under what conditions purposes can be treated as defining properties of purposively, or directionally, behaving entities. The reductivist position, as we know, is that purposes, like causes, merely create a metaphysical confusion, and in any case are not necessary for an adequate scientific description of the world. There are no irreducibly teleological facts, just as there are no irreducibly causal facts. Ostensibly directively organized be-haviour might be described by using the concept of a function, as long as it is remembered, that is, that functions are merely *accidental* properties of the objects concerned, and have nothing to do with any so-called 'inherent' purposes.

As against this view, I would like to argue—using again my earlier example—that within the biological context in which the salivary glands operate, their particular role represents their defining, not merely their accidental, characteristic. In other words, there is nothing wrong with a teleological account of their activity. On the contrary, such an account seems quite appropriate (their biological purpose is to help keep the ingestion channels in good working order). Moreover, unless it were possible to give a teleological account of what they do, it would be impossible to have a clear grasp of the ontological connection between their activity and the effect this activity has on the functioning of the system of which they are part. An account in terms of sufficient conditions is compatible with there being no such connection at all.

Now it is of course true that the function that a given thing happens to perform within a certain context is not necessarily such that it could not be performed by any other thing. Organ transplantation may cause difficulties, but in mechanical systems, in particular, a replacement of spare parts is commonplace and poses no problems. Yet it would be foolish to pretend that the function that a given object happens to play within a given context, even within a purely mechanical context, is never anything but an accidental property of that object. This implies that an object's defining properties, as distinct from its accidental properties, are independent of any role, or roles, that that object might contextually perform, and this is an absurd notion.

The point, briefly, that I wish to make is this: that objects can not significantly be said to possess properties outside and independently of any context. They don't have 'extra-contextual' metaphysical essences which remain invariant irrespective of the contextual circumstances. On the contrary, such properties as an object happens to have are inescapably context-relative, and must be counted as part of its essential description with respect to the context of which that object is a constituent element.

Let me illustrate this with a fresh example. Suppose one of the hands on my clock falls off and I manage somehow to fit a small sewing needle to replace it. It is not an ideal solution and the contraption won't work for long, but, as long as it does work, the needle performs the function of the second hand. Are we to say that its function within the context of the clock is not part of its essential description? Only the assumption that it was originally made with the *intention* to serve as a needle and the ramshackle nature of my repair job might stand in the way of its acceptance as a genuine clock hand. Someone who was not aware of its provenience and happened to believe that the amateurish look of the job was merely the manufacturer's whimsy would have no difficulty in accepting it as such.

My quartz clock qualifies as a clock only under certain specified conditions. If placed within a strong magnetic field, it no longer keeps time. If it is flattened by a heavy lorry it becomes a piece of junk metal which once was a clock. The doorknob on my door was specifically made for the purpose, but there is no intrinsic property that would prevent it from acquiring a completely different role. If I chose to fit it as a handle to my walking stick, it would no longer be a doorknob, and for all an innocent onlooker might know, it never was one. Manufacturers these days are increasingly marketing multi-purpose appliances, designed to serve a wide variety of uses. An electric motor equipped with a suitable drive shaft and enclosed in a hand-held casing can function as a drill, a sander, a power saw, a lawn-edge trimmer, and who knows what else, depending upon which attachments are used, and in what context. When its contextual function changes, so does its definition.

It is not true to say, therefore, that the various *ad hoc* uses that an object may be put to in various circumstances can never be regarded as part of its essential description. Inasmuch as the object is contextually identified by the function it performs, its function represents its definitional characteristic with regard to that context. Its essential description is not fixed once for all time. In a sense, an object acquires an identity only in respect of a context within which it accomplishes something. The lungs removed from the body and used for a different purpose are lungs in name only. My clock flattened by the heavy truck is a clock no longer.

As regards the distinction between essential and accidental propeties, this distinction clearly will depend upon which context is regarded as criterial in the given circumstances; and the nature of the criterial context, in turn, will depend, in the final analysis, upon our interests and needs.

Target States and Retrospective Explanation

So the conclusion that we seem to be inexorably driven towards is that if a satisfactory account of the possibility of change can be provided at all, then it must be in terms of 'for the sake of'. The problem of change is a problem of explaining the possibility and the structure of the transition from a state A to a state B, and this transition, as has been shown, cannot be accounted for in causal terms, or rather in terms of efficient causes supposedly producing changes *a tergo*. The progress from A to B, and the inner cohesion of the sequence, it seems, can be made sense of only by treating B as a target state and trying to understand the whole sequence backwards.

The illusion of *a tergo* explanation is nourished by the belief that agents literally have the power to produce or bring about certain states of affairs by acting in a certain manner. But this involves a misconception about the nature of actions. What this means can best be illustrated by considering a few examples.

(1) Jones closed the window. (2) He turned on the light. (3) He played a tune on the piano. Normally such statements are likely to be interpreted along the following lines: (1a) Jones pushed the window light towards the frame, turned the handle and brought it about that the window was shut. (2a) He flicked the light switch and thereby caused the light to come on. (3a) He hit the keys on the piano keyboard in a certain order and produced a tune. The idea, in short, is that by his actions he was not just setting in train certain sequences of events, but that in a sense he was making certain events happen: that he was responsible for bringing them about. This, incidentally, is why cause features prominently in considerations of legal, and even moral, guilt; even though it is recognized that 'causally responsible' does not necessarily imply 'legally responsible', let alone 'morally responsible'. (I may be causally responsible for an accident of which I am both legally and morally innocent.)

Yet, despite appearances, the explanatory paraphrases (1a), (2a), and (3a) do not reproduce exactly the meaning of the original statements. The simple causal account here clearly fails to deliver the goods. The point is that the statements (1), (2), and (3) record certain actions in terms of the results achieved. Thus if the window failed to shut, Jones would have been merely trying to shut it, or going through the motion of shutting it (possibly unaware of what he was doing). If the light failed to come on, he would have been merely flicking the switch. Similarly, if the tune failed to materialize, he would have been merely hitting the piano keys, possibly with the intention of producing a tune. Whereas the original statements, if true, provide an account of Jones's action in terms of what has actually been accomplished, and hence retrospectively, the suggested interpretative paraphrases purport to explain the results in terms of the activity invested in their production.

Change, History, and the Future

It is easy to see where the main problem lies. There is no certainty that the window will actually shut if Jones attempts to shut it, although it usually does; or that the light will come on if the switch is flicked; or that a tune will materialize if the piano keys are struck in a certain order. That these things normally do happen is no guarantee that they will happen on the next occasion; nor does the fact that they do happen explain why they should happen at all, or why individual events spaced out in time should form part of the same history. The point is that we look for ontological connections between events: we do not want to say merely that *B* as a matter of fact follows *A*, but that *A* is part of the history of *B*. Unless a sequence of events can be explained in this sense, there can be no explanation of change.

Such an explanation, however, can be achieved only by looking at a sequence of events from the point of view of the target state. An answer to the question how certain events that occur at different times can form part of the *same* history, as Zeno's antinomies showed, cannot be given in terms of efficient causes, if only because there can be no proof of the causal continuity *a tergo*. Moreover, the very idea of this type of explanation does not make clear sense, not merely because there is no absolute necessity why any event should be followed by any other, but precisely because such an approach is fundamentally incapable of providing an account of the kind of perspectival orientation without which a sequence of individual events cannot constitute itself as a unitary process of change.

But now we seem to be confronted with a different problem. It is all very well to say, it might be objected, that an explanation of change can be provided only in terms of 'for the sake of', that is, teleologically. What is needed is not just the concept of a goal but the concept of a not-yet-realized goal. All the examples given above were of realized target states, and clearly not all target states are realized, or even realizable. What is more, it is essential that it should be possible for accounts of change to be phrased in terms of not-yet-realized target states; for if such accounts could be provided only in terms of realized target states, how could we be certain that the change, or changes, concerned were indeed real changes, that is, that they occurred in real time? The point is that if there is only past time, then there is no time. If an explanation of change in terms of target states is going to work, it must be possible for target states to be in the future.

Another problem that we come up against is this. Target states, we have said, have a history. They demand the existence of certain antecedent source states. Yet how can such source states be identified as source states, and how precisely do target states come into being? In concrete terms, if *A* is a target state, then necessarily there must exist at least one state antecedent to *A*, where *A* has its historical roots. But what we need to know is just what such roots consist in, and what is involved in the actual emergence of *B*?

There is prima facie only one way of dealing satisfactorily with these problems, that is, by bringing the idea of development into the picture, and by phrasing explanations of change in terms of development. Let us now consider this approach.

5

THE IDEA OF DEVELOPMENT

THE idea of development is one of the most commonplace as well as the most powerful tools in our conceptual machinery, and it is not surprising that in various forms it has exercised a dominating influence on philosophical and scientific thinking alike. In what follows, I shall confine myself to examining whether and how this idea might be utilized to cast more light on the structure and the possibility of change. As my purpose is purely theoretical, I shall not comment on the various historical interpretations of this idea, except when necessary to illustrate my own argument.

In everyday life we associate the idea of development with a process of expansion or growth that usually, though not necessarily, leads to some sort of high point or climax, and is generally followed by a reverse process of decomposition and decay. But these are relative terms, and decay from one point of view may appear as development from another. The evolutionary curve may take any course, and, depending upon where we happen to stand, it may assume a positive or negative value. The economic or political situation, as everyone knows, may develop in either direction; whereas illness invariably develops for the worse.

I am not concerned here with such questions, but with the inner structure of the evolutionary process. If the phenomenon of change makes better sense if considered under the aspect of development, it seems, then it is because development and directiveness are conceptually linked. One cannot have a clear notion of development without also having a notion of certain potentialities being realized, and along with it the idea of forward-moving time. The notion of development epitomizes the unity of past and future. Yet, as we shall see, there are limits beyond which one cannot go in employing this notion for the purpose of clarifying change without defeating one's own objective. In particular, there can be no viable theory whereby all forms of change are treated as aspects of a single, cosmic, evolutionary process.

Nor is the notion of development much use in clarifying change if development is viewed as an observer-independent process. A theory of development couched in naturalistic terms, involving, that is, a treatment of development as a process in which the observer plays no part, or in which he is reduced to a feature of a process that in principle is supposed to be describable in its entirety in impersonal, objectivistic terms, cannot capture the dimension of future and leads ultimately to a denial of change. What often tends to be overlooked is that development is a philosophical, and not a 'scientific' category (in the narrow sense of the latter term), and that it correspondingly raises broader issues. In connection with this, it might be useful to begin by pointing out what is a fairly widespread misapprehension concerning the employment of this concept, especially in some areas of natural science.

The So-Called Theory of Evolution

A good illustration of this is provided by what is known as the Darwinian Theory of Evolution. The Theory of Evolution, especially in its modern formulation, which goes back to A. Weismann, taken literally, is a misnomer; in other words, the Theory of Evolution is not about evolution at all. What Darwin was trying to do, in essence, was something quite different. His principal aim—this cannot be sufficiently stressed—was to explain how diversity of species can emerge through natural selection, not to put forward an ontological thesis about an upward evolution of the animal and vegetable kingdoms.[1]

It was Lamarck rather than Darwin who advanced what can more appropriately be described as a 'theory of evolution'. Lamarck's assumption, as is well known, was that living organisms evolve as a result of trying to satisfy certain new needs that are forced upon them, usually, by some change in

[1] Significantly in his published work he never used the term 'evolution'. (I owe this information to Richard Dawkins.)

the environment. Thus giraffes, he surmised, gradually developed long necks by trying to reach the high foliage when the food closer to hand became scarce. Evolutionary advances invariably occur by small degrees and often take a long time to make a real difference. The acquired characteristics, such as they are, are passed on to the offspring, and, depending upon the circumstances, are added to and reinforced by succeeding generations as the latter try to cope with similar needs; or, alternatively, they are suppressed or altered by countervailing needs, if the conditions change.

What marks out Lamarck's theory as against that of Darwin is its uncompromisingly teleological tone. For although Darwin himself shared the Lamarckian view that the style of life of an animal—the use or disuse of an organ, for example—can have an effect upon the nature of that animal's offspring, he did not base his theory on the idea of a purposive drive to satisfy a given need but on the idea of natural selection. In other words, irrespective of how or why living beings acquire heritable characteristics, it is only those whom such characteristics enable to cope successfully with the exigences of life in the given environment that are likely to survive and flourish.

It is easy to see why the idea of evolution here becomes secondary. The point is this: that although natural selection may produce an advance from simpler to more complex forms of life, it does not have to do so. There is nothing in Darwin's theory to indicate that it will, let alone that it must. It is possible to conceive of a scenario in which natural selection would bring about merely a sideways diversification rather than an upward movement; what is more, given the suitable constellation of circumstances natural selection might even result in the evolutionary trend being reversed from complex to simpler organic forms. That the actual evolutionary process took the course it did was simply a matter of historical accident. In short, while the theory of natural selection may help to account for why in given circumstances certain forms of life perish while others thrive, it does not throw any light upon the question why heritable variations should occur at all, or why—looking at the overall historical picture—there have always been sufficient winning variations to produce an upward evolutionary curve, leading to ever more complex forms of life, and ending with man at its apex.

In point of fact, there are no cogent reasons why any development should have taken place at all. Thus the idea of natural selection evidently is quite compatible with the supposition that all forms of life are logically independent of each other, i.e. that all so-called development is just a sequence of discrete stationary states.[2] All of which goes to confirm yet again that the Theory of Evolution does not provide an explanation of evolution; rather it trades on the idea of evolution derived from the store of commonsense beliefs, where the idea of evolution is closely intertwined with that of growth.

Growth as a Blueprint of Development

By 'growth' I mean here principally organic growth, such as is exhibited by living organisms, including ourselves. The experience of growth, like that of decay, is part of our experience of life, and whilst prima facie there is nothing logically contradictory in the idea of living organisms being subject to neither growth nor decay, all life as we know it is characterized by both these features. Living organisms, feeding on a variety of energy sources, expand in size and complexity, usually by a process of cell division and differentiation, until they reach a certain

---

[2] There is something of a 'split-personality' syndrome in the attitude of some modern 'Weismannian' neo-Darwinists. They continue to talk about 'evolution' while at the same time arguing for a position that strictly does not require evolution at all. With regard to the question of heritability of acquired characteristics, they regard their anti-Lamarckian views as having been vindicated in particular by the developments in modern molecular biology, which seem to indicate that heredity-controlling information can be passed from nucleic acids to proteins, but not vice versa. In other words, acquired characteristics (e.g. the enlarged muscles of an athlete) do not get inscribed into the genetic code. However, if one is interested in evolution and not just in the mechanics of natural selection, one has to confront the question of the *origins* of heritable variations, viz. why and how do such variations come about? This question, to quote one writer on Darwinism, 'remains central to evolutionary biology, if only because Lamarck's theory is the only alternative to Darwin's that has been suggested' (J. M. Smith (ed.), *Evolution Now* (London and Basingstoke, 1982), 91).

biologically optimal point, after which they generally go into decline and die. Of course, the details of the whole picture are vastly more complex than this suggests, with numerous localized processes of growth and decay going on at varying pace and intensity all the time, although it is the general prevalence of one or the other of these two kinds of process in the context of the organism as a whole that determines the latter's life-cycle.

Ascription of growth involves the assumption of identity of the subject of growth over time. The organism that grows remains the 'same' organism, despite its changing attributes. The apple tree in my garden is still numerically the same tree even though it has altered beyond all recognition since it was first planted. My justification for saying this is not simply that the tree occupies the same position, or roughly the same position, as it occupied then, but the belief that its modifications through time represent a realization of certain potentialities which in an embryonic form have been part of it from the beginning.

I shall return to this question presently, especially with a view to exploring the thesis that the idea of a goal-directed realization of built-in potentialities as seemingly exemplified by the phenomenon of growth not only involves, but also helps to elucidate the idea of an enduring subject of change, i.e. that the two ideas are logically interlinked.

Consider first certain elementary features of growth, such as are familiar from textbooks of elementary biology. At the cellular level, growth occurs by cell division, cell enlargement and/or maturation, and, in some instances, by simple cell accretion.[3] In higher organisms, growth is marked by a complex process of differentiation, whereby different groups of cells assume different physiological functions and arrange themselves in certain distinctive ways to form bodily organs. The rate of growth in different parts of the organism often varies considerably. Moreover, certain cells retain the capacity for division for extensive periods, whereas others soon go through a process of dehydration and die. In plants, the replicative activity takes

---

[3] As in e.g. slime mould.

place in the most dramatic fashion in an annual cycle in meristems at the tips of stems and roots, whereas elsewhere the cells tend to replicate at a slower pace, or cease to replicate altogether and metabolically stagnate or die, as in tree bark or autumn leaves.

The key presumption underlying the above account is that of directiveness. This of course reflects the way in which we talk about growth generally, phrasing our explanatory accounts as a matter of course in teleological terms. Organic growth is always directive, even though in the particular context in which it takes place it is not necessarily functional. One particularly striking form of directive growth is the process of regeneration, of which some invertebrates, especially, provide the most spectacular examples. Thus certain species of flatworm will reproduce the complete organism from a mere fragment of their own body; and if tadpoles and salamanders should have their tails snipped off, they will happily grow new tails to replace them. The repair effected in such cases is dramatic, but the process itself is commonplace, and is instantiated by any example of healing. Thus if I cut my finger with a knife, a mechanism of directive growth is immediately triggered off, with the adjacent cells beginning to multiply and form fresh tissue to close the wound, the entire process—barring infection—advancing apace and switching itself off as soon as the repair is completed. And, of course, there are many other equally humdrum, though no less significant, examples of regeneration, such as the growth of hair, which continues long after the body has passed its metabolic peak and has started on its descending catabolic curve.

In all such cases growth is controlled and goal-directed, and the question might be, why should this *necessarily* be so? A possible counter-example that immediately leaps to mind is the ostensibly chaotic proliferation of cells in malignant tumours. Not only is such growth non-functional with regard to the body, it seems, but is totally blind and disorderly. However, this impression merely reflects the uncertainty as to whether such tumours should be regarded as being of the body, or as organisms in their own right. If they are of the body, then their growth does indeed appear chaotic and non-functional. But if, as seems more appropriate, such tumours are regarded as parasites, feeding, so to speak, upon the organism to which they are attached, then it must be accepted that their ostensibly erratic and uncontrolled behaviour, so far from being non-functional and non-directive, merely obeys their own peculiar rules of survival.

Growth and directiveness thus seem to go essentially together, although, as we are reminded by the above examples, the aspect of directiveness must not be confused with that of contextual functionality, or 'usefulness'.

Can the Idea of Growth Help to Throw Light on the Concept of Reidentifiable Particulars?

Let us now return to the question of identity of the subject of growth. In the preceding section, I have commented in a general way on the aspect of directiveness of growth. I now propose to take a closer look at the conceptual link between the idea of directiveness and the assumption of identity of the subject of growth, in order to see whether and to what extent the concept of growth might be employed to gain a clearer insight into the idea of particulars, such as those that inhabit our world, or indeed any kind of what has sometimes been called 'ontological continuants'. This obviously is of some considerable importance, if only because a teleological model based on the idea of growth seems to provide the naturalistic metaphysician with one last opportunity to produce a plausible theory of change.

In the context of everyday experience, we tend to think of empirical particulars as being individuated by the places they occupy relative to each other within a common space. This works well enough for practical purposes, but is philosophically unsatisfactory. It is unsatisfactory if only because it begs the question of the identity of places. Consider a simple example. I have two identical chairs in my room. One is by the window and the other is in front of the fireplace, and normally such place indications are accepted as a sufficient criterion of their numerical difference. But of course the places here are indicated in relation to certain things whose identity is already taken for granted. In other words, it is assumed that the identity of the window and that of the fireplace are not in dispute. But if places can be identified and numerically distinguished only relative to numerically identical things, then evidently places alone can not serve as a sufficient principle of individuation.

Consider now the question of reidentifiability of particulars. In the above, the assumption was simply that empirical particulars are individuated by the places they occupy relative to each other, wherever they happen to be, or for how long. In fact, most of the things that we come across in the ordinary course of events are relatively enduring and, in principle at least, reidentifiable. The chair by the window is numerically, not just qualitatively, identical with the chair I was sitting on a short while ago. During the half an hour or so that has elapsed since then, it has no doubt undergone a series of imperceptible changes, but it has not altered its identity. The paperweight on my desk is the same paperweight that I bought in an antique shop three years ago. The portrait that hangs on the wall opposite is an original, not a copy. And of course I have not changed my own identity, despite my greying hair.

Notice that I am talking here not of the criteria of reidentification, but of the idea of temporally extended, and hence in principle reidentifiable, particulars. It is sometimes assumed that if the idea of such ontological continuants is to make clear sense at all, then it is only provided that there are criteria available whereby in given circumstances it can be actually established whether two separately observed particulars are numerically the same; but this is an error. The intelligibility of the idea of existentially unique yet enduring ontological items does not depend upon the availability of foolproof criteria of reidentification. It is questionable whether there can be anything remotely approaching foolproof criteria of reidentification, but this does not render the idea of enduring particulars unintelligible or meaningless.[4]

Moreover, without postulating the existence of some such ontologically enduring items it is impossible to account for the

---

[4] I have discussed this problem at length in my book *The Concept of Reality* (London, 1986). See ch. 3.

possibility of objective change. Yet what does make the idea of such items meaningful? Or, to phrase it in another way, what justifies the assumption that different, including incompatible, attributes can be predicated of the same subject over time? What makes such an assumption intelligible?

It is here that the idea of growth might provide some useful conceptual enlightenment. Ascription of growth, as was emphasized earlier on, involves the supposition of an enduring subject of growth. But perhaps the idea of an enduring subject *itself* requires the idea of growth before it can make clear sense? Perhaps the two ideas are logically interdependent? If this is so, then surely by studying the structure of growth we can at the same time gain a better understanding of what is involved in positing temporally extended, reidentifiable ontological items.

Translated into more concrete terms, the above view might be expressed as follows. Organic growth is a process whereby a certain genetic design encoded in cellular chromosomes is brought to fulfilment. Moreover, every cell of the organism, irrespective of the specific stage of development that the organism in question has reached, retains the original genetic blueprint and can in principle be used for cloning other, similar organisms. Even though the organism develops and alters its appearance, it carries its genes with it unaltered for as long as it remains in existence. It may replace all of its cells, but it does not change its genetic fingerprint. Its informational base, encoded in its DNA, remains the same. It is only when this base becomes eroded that its identity goes.

At the same time, the organism is subject to a continuous process of change. In particular, change as effected by growth is a means whereby the individual's genetic code replicates itself and ensures its own survival by manufacturing for itself a biologically differentiated cellular body which will the better withstand the rigours of a hostile environment. It pursues the policy of self-preservation and self-perpetuation, and in order to achieve its objective it has to initiate a process of change, and modify and adapt, according to need. By contrast, in an inanimate object there is no natural, built-in mechanism that might be seen as providing a linkage between any two successive stages in its existence.

Here, then, it seems, we might have an answer to our problem. If clarification is required of what is involved in the idea of an enduring subject capable of taking incompatible predicates over time, surely all that is needed is to point to growing organisms. What is more, there may even seem to be some merit in going further still, and claiming that it is the living organisms themselves that represent the basic particulars and the only enduring subjects of change.

Is All Change an Aspect of Development?

What the above amounts to is a rough outline of what at first glance, at any rate, appears to be a more promising naturalistic theory of change. The various possibilities of the naturalistic treatment of the concept that we have considered so far all seemed to come to grief. Might not an approach based on the idea of a living entity be made to work?

I shall try to answer this question by broadening its scope, that is, by phrasing it in terms of growth-like, organic development generally. Consider the salient points of the above argument. The concept of change demands an enduring subject of change. The idea of an enduring subject of change can be made clear only with reference to a subject of growth. Growth, however, is a form of development. The inference, therefore, that suggests itself is that, ultimately, change in all its forms can be made fully intelligible only if it can be treated as an aspect of development. Let us see whether this in fact is a philosophically sustainable position.

It certainly is not a *novel* position. That all change is explicable in terms of development has been argued often enough in the past. The evolutionary conception of reality was a well-entrenched philosophical notion long before evolutionary ideas began to invade areas of empirical science. It is an attractive notion with strong visionary overtones that many religiously inspired metaphysical thinkers in particular have found difficult to resist. However, the theoretical difficulties involved in assimilating all change to development, unsurprisingly, are formidable, and, as we shall see presently, in a naturalistic context lead to a negation of change. Let us begin with some preliminary general observations.

'Development' (as I am here using the term) is generally understood to represent a process of unfolding of certain traits or features that have been present only in a latent form hitherto. Or, to use the traditional idiom, it is a process whereby certain potentialities that inhere in the subject of development are realized or brought to fruition. The reasons why such processes should occur at all, or the circumstances of their occurrence, need not detain us at the moment. Development in a given case may be triggered off by any number of factors; what matters is that when it does take place, certain inchoate traits of the developing subject are made manifest that, albeit dormant, have been there from the start. The seed has the capacity for growth which it may or may not realize if put in the ground. But, irrespective of whether it does realize it, such capacity remains part of its essential description.

This explanation is not entirely satisfactory. There are a number of difficulties that need to be ironed out before it can be made to work. To begin with, development involves more than just a realization of certain inherent capacities. When the spring regains its normal size after being compressed and released, it realizes its power of elasticity, but no development has taken place, even though the power of elasticity does represent the spring's defining property, that is, it forms part of its essential description. It is part of the definition of the litmus paper that it has the capacity to change from blue to red if inserted into acid, and back to blue if dipped into alkali, but the paper does not develop as it does so. Evidently the realization of a capacity that happens to be part of the essential description of the changing subject does not always or necessarily represent a case of development.

But, quite apart from this, there are changes that do not seem to involve a realization of any capacities that may be reasonably thought to form part of the essential description of the object in question. When my kitchen scales record weight as their spring is depressed by a load in the tray, the resulting change of state of the scales represents a realization of a capacity that may be regarded as part of their essential description (*qua* scales). But that the scales happen to be on the right-hand side of the cooker, or that they are painted white, or that they were given to me as a present last Christmas has nothing to do with their essential description, and if I should transfer them to another place, or alter their relational properties by simply switching the position of the kitchen furniture around them, or paint them another colour, or give them away to someone else, none of these changes could be reasonably claimed to involve any of the scales' definitional, as distinct from what might be called their incidental, capacities.

What is important to note is this: that however such changes may be categorized, they certainly cannot be said to represent instances of development. Development does involve a realization of certain capacities, but it does not reduce to a realization of certain capacities. It is rather a process whereby the developing subject undergoes certain structural changes and expands the range of its powers in a particular direction as it advances towards a given goal, or target state, with all the successive stages of the evolutionary process being closely interlinked.

So the conclusion seems to be that either we shall have to abandon the attempt to explain all change in terms of development, or else we shall have to try and devise a method whereby it might be possible to rephrase the references to inessential or merely extrinsic changes such as those mentioned above in terms of the development of some *other* entities that are possibily ontologically more basic. The difficulty with the first alternative, of course, is that we are back to square one: that is, we are faced with the familiar problem of how to devise a satisfactory universal model that would enable us to account for all forms of change. If, on the other hand, we opt for the second alternative, then we are confronted with the difficulty of constructing convincing paraphrases that would allow us to claim that it is certain other entities, rather than those that seem to be directly involved, that are really being talked about.[5]

---

[5] Leibniz's theory of self-developing monads as the basic ontological entities might be seen as an attempt to provide an account of change along the above lines.

Existential Change and Monism versus Pluralism

As it happens, even if it were possible to achieve the latter aim, that is, even if we succeeded in devising a method for producing the required paraphrases, our difficulties would still not necessarily be at an end. For, unless our evolutionary basic entities were not just relatively enduring but imperishable, there would still remain the problem of *existential* change to contend with. The point is this: that given such entities come into and go out of existence, then—on the hypothesis that all changes are forms of development—it must be possible to account for such existential changes in terms of development too. Yet whose development? It is difficult to see how such a question could be answered in any way other than by postulating a single, enduring, universal subject of development that embraces all reality.

So the conclusion is that if the basic subjects of predication are susceptible to existential change, then, on the hypothesis that all changes are forms of development, such subjects *cannot be basic*, and pluralism becomes an indefensible position. I hasten to add that I am talking here of the naturalistic, or metaphysical, pluralism of things rather than the pluralism of selves (which will be discussed in the next chapter). As is clear from my earlier comments on the matter (see Chapter 3), the thesis that I am espousing is that on naturalistic premises, the pluralist thesis becomes difficult to defend, whether the basic subjects of predication (and hence basic constitutents of reality) are interpreted as changing and perishable, or as eternal and impervious to change.

The latter view, that they are eternal and impervious to change, is of course reminiscent of classical metaphysical atomism, which involved an attempt to account for change in terms of mere displacement and rearrangements of just such basic elements. But, as we saw, any such mechanistic theory of change is doomed from the start, if only because it is unable to account for how any such ontological item can acquire a succession of incompatible predicates as it enters or leaves the various atomic clusters without forfeiting its own identity. If

change can be made sense of at all, it seems, our basic subjects
of predication, at the very least, must be capable of internal
development. Yet, on naturalistic premises, this view too runs
into trouble, and it soon becomes obvious that the thesis that
there can be a plurality of such items cannot be plausibly
sustained.

It is not difficult to see why this is so. All such items must be
logically independent of each other, that is, each of them must
be such that its essential description cannot form an integral
part of the essential description of any of the others. Unless they
are logically independent of each other they can not qualify as
basic subjects of predication. Logical independence and 'basic-
ness' go hand in hand.

Now this is not how the world usually appears to ordinary
common sense. In general we tend to take the view that all
things and events around us are interconnected, even though
their connections often may not be very obvious, and are
indeed sometimes very remote and tenuous. No thing, we feel,
is possessed of such self-sufficiency that it could survive, let
alone be adequately described in isolation from everything else
in the universe. There is a complex pattern of causal interaction
linking everything with everything else, and complete logical
independence is an absurdity.

Things begin to look different only if the world is taken as a
whole. Consider, for example, the case of a cosmologist who
treats the universe as a single, large particular. From his point of
view, it is quite in order to say that, while all things in the
universe are logically interdependent, the universe as a whole
does not depend upon anything external to itself. Provided his
assumption that the universe can be treated as a single entity is
granted—and, within a naturalistic context anyway, there are
no prima facie reasons for dismissing such a hypothesis as in
principle untenable[6]—then clearly the description of the uni-

---

[6] If there were, a good number of modern cosmologists would be out of a job.
It should be emphasized that the above hypothesis has nothing to do with the
kind of anthropomorphism attacked by Hume in his *Dialogues Concerning
Natural Religion*. Hume was merely concerned that the universe should not be
confused with a machine that 'arose from design'.

verse as logically independent must be accepted as meaningful, although it need not be true.

This at once helps to focus attention upon what is the key issue in the monism-versus-pluralism controversy. If the principle that whatever qualifies as a basic subject of predication must be logically independent (in the sense explained earlier) is taken seriously, then it is difficult to see how it can be intelligibly claimed that there could be more than one such subject in existence. For if there were more than one such entity, then there could be nothing in the essential description of any of them that would point to, or presuppose, the possibility, let alone the existence, of the others. The principle of logical independence thus seems most naturally to lead to the position of ontological monism.

The Idea of a Universal Subject of Development

In sum, if all change is to be interpreted as an aspect of development, then, it appears, we have no option but to postulate a single, universal subject of development. For if the world were made up of a plurality of such evolutionary subjects, they would have to be mutually logically independent as well as imperishable; and, as we have seen, this position is hard to defend with plausible arguments.

But consider the monistic option: does the supposition of a single, universal subject of development represent a philosophically more viable alternative? In a sense, the difficulties engendered by the notion of a single, universal subject of development are more severe still. To some extent these difficulties echo those that we encountered in our discussion of universal substance in Chapter 3, despite the ostensible difference between the two notions. The central issue remains that of identity. The universal substance is supposed to represent the enduring, single substratum of the phenomenal manifold. But, as we saw, such a substratum cannot exist independently of the manifold, and, if so, then the talk of an underlying substratum is misleading. The fact, if it happens to be a fact, that certain objects—or all objects, for that matter—have certain traits in common does not warrant the inference that they are all made of the same stuff. 'Stuff' here is just a metaphor for 'common concept'.

So the question is: what meaning, if any, can be attached to the claim that a universal substance represents the basic identical subject of change? What is it that remains identical? And, furthermore, how can such a substance give rise to the perceptual diversity of appearances that are supposed to represent its modifications?

It is clear that if 'substance' here is to be conceived as the basic material underlying the perceptual diversity of appearances, then it necessarily remains a hazy concept which does nothing to help to resolve the problem of the possibility of change. It is precisely for this reason that some philosophers have tried to replace the concept of a universal substance by that of a 'universal subject'; or rather to interpret universal substance in the sense of a universal subject. If the idea of change as an acquisition of incompatible attributes over time is to be made intelligible at all, they have argued, the concept of substance has to be modified to conform to the idea of a subject of development. Whereas the idea of a universal substance necessarily remains obscure, the identity of the universal subject of development derives from the latter's inherent purpose.

Yet what is its purpose, and why is development needed to achieve it? What does the universal subject represent, if anything, above and beyond its phenomenal manifestations (or attributes)? How does the diversity of the phenomenal world come into being? Questions begin to proliferate at this point, and philosophically plausible answers are precious few. Attempts have sometimes been made to cope with these difficulties by ascribing the emergence of the phenomenal manifold to a deliberate act whereby the universal subject of development engages in a process of realization of its own inherent potentialities. If conceived in this sense, the whole process acquires a familiar theological connotation. But for reasons that I shall explain presently, as a universal theory of change it does not—nor indeed can it—work.[7]

[7] The problem of explaining the need of the self-identical universal subject to 'manifest' itself in phenomenal emanations has always troubled the pantheistic,

A Universal Theory of Development and the Possibility of Change

It cannot work because basically it is still in the grip of a naturalistic bias and is incapable, in virtue of its underlying assumption that the world can in principle be described in its totality, of giving a satisfactory account of time. The point, briefly, is that no such universal theory of development can throw any light on development as a process from past to future, and, in a sense, it is not about development at all. It follows that, if change is to be explained in terms of development, then such a theory has nothing to say about change either. Essentially any such theory suffers from three major drawbacks.

First, it invariably ends up by treating development as a closed system. Moreover, its account of development is necessarily an account of a process that in essentials has already been completed, or, at the very least, is such as enters its closing phase with the construction of the theory itself. The point is that the logic of the whole process cannot be fully grasped except from the point of view of its goal, and the goal cannot be known until it is reached. This follows from the nature of the goal, which is an objective end state, not a subjective intention. If the end state was not reached, it could as little be an object of knowledge as tomorrow's facts can be an object of knowledge. In addition, if the goal were still in the future, there would be no certainty that when it materialized it would represent the

or near-pantheistic, believers in universal evolution. Plotinus (to cite one example) speaks of the phenomenal manifold of the empirical world as coming into being as a result of an 'overflowing' or 'superabundance' of 'the One', whatever that means. In the *Enneades* he explains his view of the act of creation thus: '*The One* is all things and not a single one of them: it is the principle of all things, not all things . . . How then do all things come from the One, which is simple and has in it no diverse variety, or any sort of doubleness? It is because there is nothing in it that all things come from it: in order that being may exist, the One is not being, but the generator of being. This, we may say, is the first act of generation: the One, perfect because it seeks nothing, has nothing, and needs nothing, overflows, as it were, and its superabundance makes something other than itself. This, when it comes into being, turns back upon the One and is filled, and becomes Intellect by looking towards it' (with English trans. by A. H. Armstrong (Cambridge, Mass. and London, 1966), V. ii. 59). This is not very inspired or imaginative, even as poetry.

last event of a temporally continuous evolutionary process, rather than being an independent event temporally unconnected with what went on before. Furthermore, there is always the possibility that whatever happens to be posited as the final goal might turn out not to be the final goal at all. A theory of universal development, however, cannot account for such a possibility; that is, it cannot account for the possibility of its own failure. Its claim to truth is unconditional. At the same time, the emergence of the theory itself must be explicable in terms of the theory. For if it was not, the theory would be in an important sense incomplete. But the emergence of the theory cannot be explained in terms of the theory without relating its emergence to the end state of the process that the theory purports to depict. A universal theory of development is thus necessarily an exercise in *retrospective* explanation. But, as we saw earlier on, a retrospective account of events is not necessarily an account of a temporal sequence. If viewed from the end result backwards, the development might easily not have been a process in time at all.

A second major problem to which a universal theory of development gives rise is this. Given the teleological premises of such a theory, its success depends on its being able to explain why the given sequence of events has produced the result that it has rather than any other. What it must show, in other words, is that the given process follows a certain direction not just as a matter of fact but of necessity. But how can this be shown? How can it be shown that state *B* necessarily follows state *A*? Now, conceivably it might be argued that *A* and *B* are conceptually related in such a way that the occurrence of *A* logically demands the occurrence of *B*. But this won't solve the problem, for logical relationships have nothing to do with temporal order, and it is the latter that we are interested in. What is demanded is not merely that when *A* occurs, *B* should occur also, but that they should occur in a temporal sequence. Given the usual meaning of 'swimming', it is logically impossible to swim without making waves, but these two events occur simultaneously not successively, and there is no contradiction in one event ceasing when the other does. The point is that there is no inevitability about progress, and hence no inevitability of the goal in terms of which the theory articulates its explanation of development.

Thirdly, there is the problem of deciding the identity of the subject of development: who or what develops? Most theories of universal development are theological in character, that is, they postulate a cosmic agency which is said to 'externalize' itself in the phenomenal world in order to fulfil itself by realizing its own potentialities.[8] But the original blueprint for such a cosmic subject lies of course in the notion of the human self, and it is easily seen that the latter notion breaks down under the weight of the task assigned to it, if it is made to embrace the whole of reality. A universal subject is essentially outside time, and an agency outside time is an incoherent notion. If, however, the universal subject cannot be coherently conceived as an agent, then it is reduced to the manifold of its alleged 'manifestations', and we are left with the problem of how such 'manifestations' are related to each other, and how in such a world there can be change or development at all.

---

[8] Hegel, as is well known, assigned such a cosmic role to what he called the 'Absolute Spirit'. In the more mundane Marxist version of Hegel the place of the Absolute Spirit is taken by historical humanity, which is presented as the subject of development. But this is a vague notion and hardly an improvement on Hegel. The point is that there is no collective, let alone individual, will that might be supposed to carry the development forward—Marxists are no 'voluntarists'—and if the development of humanity is controlled by economic forces, then humanity strictly is no longer the subject but the object of the historical process, even though the progress-governing forces are generated by its own activity, in particular the activity of 'production'.

6

CHANGES AND SELVES

IF all change, including existential change, is to be explained in terms of development, then, as we have just seen, there is no ready alternative to interpreting development as a comprehensive cosmic process, and yet this immediately gives rise to paradoxes about time and destroys the very basis of the intelligibility of change. We thus seem to have reached an impasse. The philosophical evolutionary model was intended not only to help to sweep clean any remaining difficulties that lingered on in the ruins of the mechanistic account of change but in particular to provide a more secure footing for a teleological approach by equipping it with a refurbished concept of a not-yet-realized target state within the context of an objective, forward-moving time. As it turned out, the project misfired, and as a result the perplexity about the whole issue increased rather than diminished.

In a sense, given the naturalistic tenor of the whole enterprise, a different outcome could hardly have been expected. The metaphysical theories of development in their various forms merely represent the farthest point that can be attained by travelling along the naturalistic route. With the problem of clarifying the rationale of change thus remaining unresolved one is left with no option but to retrace one's steps and try out a different kind of strategy. To this end, it seems, the best place to start is the notion of a temporally extended self. Phenomenologically the self embodies the idea of change, in that the combined notions of variation and persistence through time represent an instrument of its own self-understanding. I should stress that I am here talking of 'our' kind of self, not about selfhood in general. (I wish to reserve my judgement about the characteristics of selfhood in general for the time being.) This phenomenological self knows itself *qua* self inasmuch as it knows itself as a subject of memory beliefs, of acts of perception, and acts of anticipation. Moreover, an essential component of its own self-understanding, I shall maintain, is the idea of other selves, in this sense: that it is only with a reference to other selves that a significant distinction can be made between the what-seems-to-me-to-be-so and the what-is-so type of claim. In particular, there is a direct logical link between the self's targeting itself *qua* temporally extended in real time, that is, as having a real and not just an imagined or dreamt past, and the idea of other selves.

I shall argue, accordingly, that it is here that we must seek our clues in trying to clarify the idea of change. Naturalism being incapable of throwing any light on the problem, the only available option, it seems, is to proceed through a phenomenological exploration of the self. However, the road ahead is not entirely free from obstacles. What we shall have to concentrate on first is a clarification of the conditions of the intelligibility of change. But intelligibility does not necessarily entail reality, and, as we shall see, there are some further sceptical arguments that will have to be dealt with before the sceptic can finally be beaten off and forced to withdraw into ignominious silence.

Selves and Persons

It is necessary, to begin with, to draw a distinction between selves and persons. In what follows, I shall concern myself exclusively with the phenomenological concept of a self, not with the concept of a person. Consequently, I shall not be discussing questions such as: What are the criteria of personal identity? Is being a self a sufficient, or even necessary, condition of being a person? To what extent, if any, does personal identity depend upon bodily identity? Etc.

The assumption underlying such questions is that persons are ontological items 'out there', as it were, whose properties are specifiable in the third person, and the central problem, accordingly, is seen as being one of deciding just what the distinguishing properties of such items are. But the naturalistic inspiration of such an approach is at the same time its greatest handicap and there is not much likelihood of one arriving at any firm position by pursuing the indicated route. As always,

problems abound, and the criteria for evaluating proposed
solutions are uncertain. For how do we decide between the rival
theories of 'personhood'? Can the ontological items in question
be defined exclusively in terms of mental attributes; and if yes,
what kind of mental attributes? Or do persons necessarily take
physical as well as mental predicates? And, assuming the latter
is the case, is it possible for different persons to share the same
physical predicates, for example, to inhabit the same body; or,
conversely, for the same person to inhabit different bodies,
either simultaneously or in succession? Or is it rather that
bodily identity is presupposed by personal identity, in such a
way that the existential uniqueness and continuity of the
person is inseparably tied up with the existential uniqueness
and continuity of the body?

All these issues have been endlessly lucubrated and argued
about, especially in recent philosophy, with the debate invariably
generating more fog than light. Which seems to indicate that
there is something radically wrong with the way such issues are
being addressed. Ostensibly the position easiest to criticize is
that persons *qua* persons are characterized exclusively by
mental attributes. If this were true, so the familiar argument has
it, then any ascription of physical predicates to oneself would
become unintelligible. I could not say, for example, 'I have grey
hair' as well as 'I feel sorry for myself' (let alone that I feel sorry
for myself on account of my grey hair) and claim that in both
cases I am speaking of the same I; which is patently absurd. But
notice that this objection presupposes—does not explain
why—the logical subject in the two cases is the same; in other
words, it presupposes the very view that the dualist rejects.

The dualist's position is that the situation in the two cases is
different, in that the subject of the first of the two statements
quoted above is my body. What is being said, the dualist
argues, is that my body, or rather a specific part of the body
'attached' to me, has grey hair; and the circumstance that I do
have a body is merely a contingent matter; that is, I would not
be any the less of a person for not having it, even though I
would most certainly be one of a different sort. This may not be
a tenable position, but it takes more than a simple appeal to
common sense to show that it is not.

In point of fact, even if we concede that possession of physical as well as mental attributes is a necessary precondition of being a person, our problems are by no means at an end. For the question that has to be answered is, just what kind of physical, and what kind of mental attributes? At what stage of his/her development precisely does a human being qualify as a person? Is there a sense in which personhood might be justifiably ascribed to higher animals, but not, say to human embryos, or newly born babies? And—to mention one particularly delicate topic—in what sense exactly can the status of a person be accorded to a severely retarded or brain-damaged individual?

Evidently there is a wide scope for disagreement about all this, and very little prospect of hammering out a generally agreed position. Part of the trouble undoubtedly lies in the failure to differentiate clearly between the aspect of selfhood and that of personhood. 'What constitutes a person?' and 'What constitutes a self?' are two very different questions, and demand correspondingly different types of treatment. The concept of a person, I think, is best seen as a sociological category, with persons, at the most general level, being treated as subjects of rights, on the understanding that a subject of rights may but need not be a self. This, admittedly, involves accepting among persons a vast array of sentient beings, ranging from lower to higher forms of life and occupying different positions on the scale of rights within the given social context, but the advantage of taking such an approach is that it makes it that much easier to differentiate the issues surrounding the concept of personal identity from the more fundamental philosophical problems of selfhood.

However, I do not propose to go into the details of this question now. Nor do I propose to concern myself specifically with the problem of personal identity, or the question of what attributes a sentient being must have to qualify as a subject of rights (clearly, if the above approach is accepted, this will inevitably have to be a contextual decision, depending upon the relevant circumstances and the prevailing social standards). Rather I shall concern myself with the conditions under which attributes can be meaningfully ascribed to any ontological item at all; and in particular with the question of what is involved in ascribing incompatible attributes to such items. In other words, I shall be concerned with exploring the conditions of the possibility of change; or, phrased in the idiom of traditional metaphysics, with the possibility of *becoming*. Such conditions, as I have already emphasized, cannot be defined in purely naturalistic terms, but demand rather—initially, at any rate—a phenomenological investigation of the self, that is, a descriptive analysis of the self from the self's own point of view. I say 'initially' because there will be a point, in particular when we come to consider the conditions of objectivity, when it will be necessary to go beyond the confines of the phenomenologically given, in the narrow sense of the latter term, and postulate not just the possibility but the existence of a plurality of inter-communicating selves that are all logically—though (as a rule) not empirically—independent of each other.[1]

Self-Attribution of Experiences

What, then, is a self, and how might an analysis of the notion of self help in clarifying the possibility of objective change? Phenomenologically the self comes into being through an act of self-attribution of experiences, and a concomitant act of differentiation between past, present, and future in a biographical time series. An act of self-attribution, in the sense in which I shall be using the term, represents an act of consciousness, and is not to be confused with an act of verbal self-ascription of an experience. An act of verbal self-ascription may but need not necessarily indicate an act of reflective appropriation; and it is the latter aspect that matters.

It is generally accepted that on most occasions one is not explicitly aware of one's experiences as forming part of a biographical time series. Just now I rubbed my elbow to remove the acute feeling of discomfort and fatigue caused no doubt by leaning on it too long while working at my desk. But I did this

---

[1] The distinction is important, for—to give an example—although it is an empirical fact that I have been brought into being by my parents, this is not a logically necessary condition of my existence *qua* self.

mechanically, and the sensation, at the time it occurred, though subliminally noted, was not reflectively, or self-consciously noted. Not only was there no reflective awareness of the subject of the experience. There was not even the minimal indexical awareness of place or time; that is, no apperception of the 'here' or 'now' of the experience. The level of awareness involved was no higher than that in, say, taking a swipe at an insect gyrating around my head.

I may or may not make use of language on such occasions. If I do, it need not necessarily make any difference. Thus while rubbing my elbow I might utter any angry word or use an elliptical sentence (which a bystander would have no difficulty in associating with my mental state) without myself being reflectively aware either of the bearer of the experience, or the time or place of its occurrence. I might just utter an inarticulate sound of pain, or cry 'Ouch', or 'Blast', or employ a more elaborate as well as syntactically more explicit expression, with or without indexical particles. None of this necessarily is an indication that I understand what I am saying or that I have a clear grasp of the experience as an event in my own biography. It is only when the indexical consciousness enters the experience that things begin to acquire a different complexion. Thus, whereas in earlier cases, despite the linguistic articulations, I was merely subliminally reacting to the event without actually registering it as an 'instance of change, with the emergence of the indexical consciousness of place and time I am already noting its co-ordinates. In consequence, indexical expressions now come to play a vital role in my verbal report. Thus, if asked, I might say 'It hurts *right here*', or 'It feels *better now*', with a deliberate emphasis on 'right here' and 'better now'.

Such emphases, as a rule, signal the presence of a high level of reflective attention. Nevertheless, prima facie at least, there still does not seem to be anything that could reasonably be described as an act of self-attribution of the experience, and it might be thought, therefore, that it is possible to have a grasp of change without necessarily having the idea of self.

Indexical Adverbs and Self-Consciousness

I shall dispute this. But, before I give my reasons, consider briefly one further point that conceivably might be cited in favour of the above view. 'It hurts here' or 'It feels better now', it might be said, like 'It is cold here' and 'It is now raining', despite the presence of indexical adverbs, cannot be treated on a par with subject/predicate sentences. On a superficial level, they might be pressed into a subject/predicate form, but *logically* they lack a proper subject, if only because the adverbs 'here' and 'now' are really pseudo-designators. They are apt to change their meaning with the speaker and the conditions of utterance. As modal terms, they cannot be compared to nouns and noun phrases, which are the only proper vehicles of ontological reference. It follows that in sentences like those above there is no entity, and certainly no self, that might reasonably be claimed to represent the logical subject 'talked about'.

This is not entirely true. There is no question, of course, that such indexical adverbs cannot be treated on a par with nouns or noun phrases; nevertheless, it does not follow that on any given occasion of their use nothing very clear can be put in their place. Thus 'here' in 'It hurts here' contextually unmistakably refers to my elbow, and 'now' happens to be 4 p.m. (our time). This, I hasten to add, is not to say that such adverbs are eliminable altogether—I have already argued (see Chapter 3) that they are not—merely that *contextually* (usually with the help of demonstratives and other indexicals) they can be given a more precise reference.

Be this as it may, the central question that remains surely is this: can sentences containing such indexicals be understood independently of the phenomenological notion of the self?— and the answer to this question must be no.

It is not difficult to see why the answer must be no. 'Here' is where 'my' elbow is, where 'I' happen to stand, in 'my' close vicinity, in 'our'—'your' and 'my'—shared neighbourhood. None of these personal and possessive pronouns would make clear sense without the conception of self. This of course is even more true of temporal indexical adverbs. Conceptually 'now' cannot be divorced from 'before now' and 'after now'. The pain I had in my elbow (= before now) is now gone, but if I continue leaning on it, it is likely to return (= after now). The intelligibility of any one of these temporal determinations is dependent upon the intelligibility of all three, and this presupposes the idea of a unity of biographical time extending from past to future; and hence the idea of self. By the 'unity of biographical time' I mean here the unity of phenomenological, or, as I have sometimes found it convenient to call it, 'indexical' time. Time, in a phenomenological context, has sometimes been said to represent a series of advancing 'nows', succeeding each other and receding into the unretrievable past. But this characterization already presupposes an understanding of what it is for a series of 'nows' to form part of the same history. In a sense, the idea of 'now' demands for its own intelligibility the idea of a unity of biographical time, in a similar way to which the idea of a natural number requires the conception of a unitary set of integers governed by the successor function and theoretically extending into infinity.

Self-Attribution of Experiences and the Idea of Change

What I am suggesting is that a general condition of the intelligibility of any form of change is that it should be possible to attribute, or reflectively appropriate, certain states or experiences to oneself as part of one's own biography, and that, therefore, the notion of self (*qua* extended in unidirectional time) is fundamental.

Consider more closely the mechanics of such acts of self-attribution. I am now retrospectively attributing to myself (or reflectively appropriating) the painful sensation in my elbow in an act of memory, and assigning it a place in a biographical series. The aching sensation occurred *before* now, and *after* I had spent some time leaning on my elbow on my desk. I become conscious of the time lapse by recollecting the more recent experiences that have displaced it. In reflectively appropriating the experience, I am at the same time including it in my own personal history and assigning it the appropriate temporal predicate. My verbal report, accordingly, will now be more detailed. Thus I might say: 'A moment ago, just before I rubbed my elbow, I felt a sharp twinge of pain, which is now gone.'

If the sensation is still continuing, my act of self-attribution will place it accordingly in my biographical present; yielding, if required, an appropriate present-tense statement. The sensation is occurring now, concurrently with my apperception of it. But this 'now' is not a tenseless contemporaneity, but an integral part of my biographical time that moves from past to future. The sensation is there now, and some time later it is there still; the subsequent 'now' being co-temporal with some other supervening experience (the hearing of the ticking of the clock, say) that overlaps the sensation in question. Or, alternatively, the painful sensation might fade out altogether for a time and re-emerge at a later point, now no longer as the same 'experience token', i.e. numerically the same, but as a different token of the same type, or specifically the same. The idea of temporal progression thus involves the idea of a sequential displacement of unique, and partially overlapping, experience *tokens*.

So phenomenologically the situation seems to be as follows. The possibility of change demands certain acts of self-attribution (or reflective appropriation) of experiences *qua* unrepeatable experience tokens within a biographical context. The self through its own acts of appropriation constitutes itself as a unity of past, present, and future within a biographical series, the differentiation between the different temporal modes being an integral part of the experience of the unity of time as 'my' time.[2]

Self-Attribution of Contradictory Predicates

Yet clearly self-attribution of experiences, or anything else, for that matter, alone, is not necessarily going to give us all we need. Above, we have taken for granted that acts of self-

[2] On the concept of the unity of biographical time see my book *The Concept of Reality*, ch. 7.

attribution take place in time; and so as a matter of fact they do. But why must they do so *necessarily*? Is it not at least conceivable that they might *not* involve the idea of time? What I have in mind is a situation in which the self-attribution of properties (be they experiences or anything else) signifies a logical rather than a temporal relation, and is therefore consistent with the notion of an extra-temporal self (such as one might associate with a supernatural being, for example). Admittedly it may be difficult to make clear phenomenological sense of such a self (phenomenological notions being modelled on our own experience); nevertheless, on the face of it, at least, the notion of an extra-temporal self does not seem to be logically incoherent.[3]

What is required, in short, is not just the general idea of self-attribution of properties but the idea of self-attribution of contradictory properties, for it is only with the latter idea that time of necessity enters the picture. One can possess any number of properties without being temporally extended, but one cannot have contradictory, or incompatible, properties. What is more, the converse might be said to hold too, in that it is only in virtue of appropriating contradictory properties that the self constitutes itself as a 'continuant', that is, as a particular that endures through time.

We now have all the essential ingredients of change. The self acts as numerically the same bearer of contradictory properties; as such, it provides a blueprint for ascription of properties, including logically incompatible properties, to any object, and supplies the basic conceptual resources for elucidating the structure of change in general. In a sense, the self *qua* self-constituting continuant might be said to represent a paradigmatic subject of change.

Moreover, in constituting itself as an enduring subject of (contradictory) properties the self necessarily projects itself into an objective realm by making itself its own topic. What I am suggesting in fact is that the self-attribution of contradictory

---

[3] This, as we shall see, is one of the main arguments in the sceptic's armoury. However, the attempt to use this argument to undermine the belief in the reality of time fails in the end. I shall have more to say about this in ch. 7.

properties, the idea of own-extendedness-in-time, and the idea of objective reference are all logically interlinked.

(Notice, incidentally, that the word 'I' as employed in self-analyses of this sort is inherently equivocal, in that it signifies both the source and the object of reference. This feature becomes particularly apparent in the first-person singular statements that involve an emphatic reference to oneself. To adapt our earlier example: 'It is *I* whose elbow is sore'. '*I* was the one who felt discomfort earlier on; and, of course, it is the same *I* who now feels the sense of relief.' Similarly in passive constructions: 'I was given—*it was I* who was given—permission to enter the house', 'I was told—*it was I* who was told—to do the job', 'I was the one who was made to do it', etc. The self-reference is often effected less awkwardly in constructions involving the use of the accusative, for example, 'I taught myself French', 'The Committee—or whoever—nominated me for the prize', 'I only have myself to blame', etc.).

In discussing the self as a self-constituting particular and an enduring subject of change I have deliberately avoided the issue of reidentification. The simple reason is that there is very little that can be said about reidentification at this stage. What requires clarification to begin with is not the conditions of reidentification, but rather the origins of the idea of identity without which a question about the conditions of reidentification would not even be intelligible. Some philosophers (Hume, for example) approach the issue of identity in a manner that seems to suggest that the idea of an identical self could make sense only provided the criteria were available for deciding how two non-contemporaneous experiences, *A* and *B*, might both be part of the 'same' biography. But this is nonsense. Unless non-contemporaneous experiences could be part of the same biography, the question about the conditions of reidentification could not even be meaningfully raised.

Unidirectionality of Biographical Time and Non-Arbitrary Order

An account of change, then, cannot be provided in isolation from the idea of self as a self-constituting continuant. This does not mean that all change is necessarily self-attributive change, or can be explained in terms of such; i.e. that, ultimately, changes in selves are the only form of becoming. Nevertheless, it does mean that one cannot significantly speak about things changing independently of the selves who posit them as changing, and hence that in assuming the existence of change one is committed to assuming the existence of selves.

I shall return to this later on. Let us now turn to another aspect of the self's self-constituting activity, namely, the idea of the unidirectional flow of biographical time, and in particular the connection between this idea and that of a non-arbitrary order.

To illustrate what is involved here, consider again the sensation of pain which, after I rubbed my elbow, gave way to a sense of relief. In reflectively appropriating this slice of my biography I am assigning the experiences in question the appropriate temporal indices. The unpleasant sensation is no longer there; it is now part of my past. It happened after I had been working at my desk for some time, and it was followed by a sense of relief when I rubbed my elbow. I recall these experiences as having happened in a certain order which cannot be retrospectively altered. Of course, I am ready to accept that I may misremember these experiences, but by the same token I am committed to the view that they cannot be retrospectively modified or switched around at will. If (as I assume) I have a past, it follows that I have an *unalterable* past.

This seems naturally to follow from the way experiences are reflectively appropriated within a biographical framework. In the act of reflective appropriation the self constitutes itself not just as a lived unity of biographical time, but as an enduring, identical subject-bearer of *forward-flowing* experiences. It was I who suffered from an irritating pain in my arm a moment ago, and it is the same I who now feels a sense of relief. The irritating pain mercifully is no longer there; it has faded into the immediate past, with a different experience having displaced it in my phenomenological present. Being part of my past, by definition it cannot recur, even though the same *kind* of experience may very well recur. Once past, it stays past. It is a unique event in a unique temporal series. Moreover, it occupies a permanent position in the series; to suppose otherwise would conflict with the notion of the irreversible forward flow of time. Given the assumption of a unidirectional order of uniquely occurring biographical events going from past to future, there is necessarily a non-arbitrary temporal order.

In other words, the fixity of the history of the self is part of the package of ideas that originate in the act whereby the self constitutes itself as a temporally extended particular. In positing myself as temporally extended, I posit myself as an identical subject of properties that once acquired cannot be disowned. If *P* is a property, then either I have had that property or I have not had that property. With regard to past time, at least, I am fully subject to the principle of the excluded middle. Either I did, or did not, feel discomfort in my arm a moment ago. What is true in respect of my past is true always; I cannot, except in fantasy, choose a different past for myself. By reflectively appropriating my experiences I am at the same time positing myself as an ontological particular with a determinate biography.

Phenomenologically, then, the idea of a temporally extended self is inseparable from that of a unidirectional flow of time, and the latter idea in turn involves the idea of history that remains beyond our control. In thinking of myself as an identical, enduring self I am at the same time projecting myself into an unretrievable past. I am acknowledging the existence of an order which I am not in a position to alter at will, and which conceivably I might misdescribe on any given occasion.

Unalterable Past, Memory, and Other Selves

From this, other important consequences follow. Thus implicit in the idea that the self has of its own unalterable past, as will become apparent presently, is the idea of *other* selves. In order to make this clear, it will be necessary to look a little more closely at the concept of memory.

Memory beliefs are an integral part of the self's idea of its own extendedness in time. Moreover, implicit in the concept of memory is the idea of an unalterable past. If past events could be arbitrarily moved round, there would be no memory, only apparent memory. Memory can be fallible, but it can also be accurate. We all have our own complaints about defective, failing, or incomplete memory, while at the same time acknowledging by implication that memory of things past can in principle be veridical and reliable. We understand the distinction between remembering and merely seeming to remember precisely because we have an idea of an unalterable past. Yet the question is, what does confer objectivity upon such an idea? What does confer objectivity upon memory statements in general?

To claim to remember that *p* is to make an implicit objectivity claim. When I say 'I remember having had coffee before starting work this morning', I am not saying that I am under the impression that I had coffee before starting to work, or that I imagine I did, but that I remember the event. Of course, there is always the possibility that I might be wrong, and that nothing of the kind took place, or that my description of the event was inaccurate (for example, that what I drank was in fact tea, not coffee). This possibility is implicit in the thesis that what I am claiming to remember belongs to an unalterable past. But if I can be mistaken about what I claim to remember, even if I don't believe I am, even if I assume that I am always right, then, it might be argued, this can be made fully intelligible only if there are certain public criteria whereby someone other than myself could in principle correct my error. If I am the only judge of whether an error has occurred, that is, if I am right whenever I think I am right, then, as Wittgenstein observed, there can be no useful concept of being right.

Objectivity and Truth

It is well to pause briefly at this point to consider this in a little more detail. There has been a good deal of confusion about the above argument in recent philosophy, partly, I think, because of a failure to draw a clear distinction between the conditions of truth and the conditions of objectivity. The conditions of truth, it should be stressed at the outset, are inseparable from the conditions of objectivity, but objectivity is not the same as truth. A proposition cannot be true without satisfying the conditions of objectivity, but clearly it is quite possible for a proposition to satisfy the conditions of objectivity and yet be false.

This confusion has tended to obscure the true meaning of the argument from error. Thus it is argued that it is conceivable that an error might occur even if no one, myself included, thought, or was able to show, even in principle, that it did. There can be uncheckable errors, it is claimed, just as there can be unverifiable truths. A proposition can be true even if it never can be seen to be so by anyone. And similarly for falsehood.

The difficulty with this reasoning, however, is that it completely overlooks the aspect of objectivity. A truth claim necessarily incorporates an objectivity claim, and this (as was pointed out above) includes memory claims: memory claims by definition incorporate objectivity claims. But this only means that we have to clarify the conditions under which such objectivity claims make sense. A necessary (though not a sufficient) condition of correctness of a memory claim is that such a claim should satisfy the conditions of objectivity, and it is the latter conditions that are in need of clarification.

I am now reminiscing again about that cup of coffee I had this morning. I drank it in a hurry and nearly spilt it over my jacket. In making this statement I am claiming by implication that the event in question forms part of my (unalterable) past. But if the claim that the said event took place in the real past rather than being merely a retrospective projection of my 'present' self is to make sense, it is necessary, as a minimum condition, that it should be possible for this claim to be understood and accepted as a genuine memory claim by other selves as well as by myself. This granted, it follows that there can be no temporally extended self unless it is possible that there should be a plurality of such selves.

Consider first the objectivity conditions in respect of truth claims generally. To assert p is at the same time to make an objectivity claim in respect of p, and such a claim has to do with the conditions that make p intersubjectively acceptable as a valid truth candidate. Obviously not every sentence can be a vehicle of a valid truth claim. 'This chair is made of wood' and

'This chair suffers from amnesia' are both grammatically unimpeachable, but the latter sentence can be accepted, at best, as a feeble joke, hardly a valid truth candidate. A truth claim in respect of *p* can be meaningfully made only on condition that *p* satisfies certain public criteria of coherence and appropriateness, and can accordingly be vetted by third persons in the light of such criteria. Such criteria are always and necessarily contextual and presuppose an institutionalized framework of social life.

However, as has already been emphasized, the conditions of objectivity are not the same as the conditions of truth, and, while it is necessary that *p* should in principle be accessible to intersubjective checks for coherence and appropriateness, the same does not necessarily apply to the evidence that makes *p* true. Thus the verifying evidence of 'This chair is made of wood' is available for anyone who cares to look. But the same is not true, or, at any rate, not nearly to the same degree, of, say, 'The sight of this chair fills me with melancholy'.[4]

Memory and the Social World

Let us now return to the concept of memory. It is clear that statements of memory too are subject to objectivity conditions, that is, they must conform to certain criteria of coherence and appropriateness. Thus I can claim meaningfully 'I remember having coffee before starting work this morning' but not, except perhaps jokingly, 'I remember having a conversation with a cup of coffee' or 'taking a bath in a cup of coffee' or 'drinking coffee from an empty cup'. None of these qualify as genuine cases of remembering.

What this shows is that there are limits to what can be coherently claimed to have occurred in the past. Such limits reflect certain intersubjectively accepted standards within the specific context within which the given statement is made. This is true irrespective of whether such claims concern publicly accessible objects or personal experiences. They are all without

---

[4] For a more detailed discussion of the conditions of objectivity see my book *The Concept of Reality*, chs. 10 and 15.

exception subject to the relevant public criteria of coherence and appropriateness.

The objectivity conditions, then, of necessity involve references to other selves. The concept of memory involves the idea of an unalterable past, and the idea of an unalterable past acquires objectivity only on the supposition that there are means whereby it can be intersubjectively decided if what I claim qualifies as a valid truth candidate. If I am the only judge as to what can or cannot have a truth value in respect of the past, then on what grounds is it to be decided that what I claim about the past is indeed about the past, i.e. that there is such a phenomenon?

Notice that this does not imply that a given memory claim is meaningful only provided it refers to a state of affairs that could have been verified at the time by independent witnesses. As was pointed out earlier on, the evidence that makes a particular memory claim true need not be wholly publicly accessible. Nevertheless, certain relevant aspects of such evidence must be publicly accessible; in particular its temporal placing must involve references to certain publicly accessible objects if the relevant memory claim is to carry the kind of objectivity claim without which it cannot qualify as a genuine memory claim at all.

Sceptical Counter-Argument: Posited and Objective Past

What I have tried to set out above are certain basic assumptions that underlie all claims about the past—the assumptions without which no such claim can qualify as a valid truth candidate. I have traced the logical connections between such assumptions in so far as the latter form part of the conception of self *qua* temporally extended in unidirectional time. But after all, it might be objected, they are precisely what it is said they are, *assumptions*, and no truth candidates that they are supposed to underpin need actually be true. What assurance do we have that all this is not just an exercise in make-believe; a devious, if convenient (and arguably unavoidable) ritual of self-deception?

That the idea of an identical yet temporally evolving self implies the idea of an unalterable past seems clear enough. But these are just conceptual links which may or may not have ontological implications. The positing of an unalterable past is one thing, its actual existence quite another. Possibly the past is just a useful fiction. If I am to have a clear conception of myself as temporally extended, evidently I must have memory beliefs and also beliefs about the future. But why should any such beliefs be *true*? What conditions must be fulfilled for them to be true?

The important point to bear in mind in this connection is that such beliefs as I may entertain about what may or may not have happened in the past, or might happen in the future, are all present-tense beliefs. I believe *now* that there was a series of events *before now*, and that there is likely to be a series of events *after now*. But surely there is no necessary link between what I believe at the present time, and what may or may not have occurred in the past, or is likely to occur in the future. Conceivably the past is just a phenomenological projection of the past, like the perspectival lines deliberately drawn on a flat surface to create an illusion of a three-dimensional body.

Thought and Time

This clearly is an objection that must be taken seriously. The sceptic conceivably might go along with our analysis of the condition of intelligibility of change, while none the less disputing the inference to its existence. His argument, in its strongest form, might run as follows.

Consider what it is to have thoughts. Thoughts as such—or what is sometimes referred to as thought-contents, or propositional contents, of acts of thinking—are atemporal; by contrast, thinking, it is generally assumed, takes place in time. Now we generally tend to equate having thoughts with thinking. Yet there is nothing intrinsically temporal in having thoughts. Having a thought, like being green, need not necessarily be an attribute with a temporal span. Nor does having two, three, or any number of thoughts, for that matter, necessarily involve time, although it presumably does. When we equate having thoughts with thinking we imagine thoughts as occurring consecutively in a temporal order as well as bearing some logical relation to each other; but that thoughts do occur consecutively, or rather that they are 'had' consecutively, is an empirical not a logical fact.

It is then at least theoretically possible to have thoughts in an atemporal fashion; in other words, having thoughts does not include time as a logical requirement. And clearly this must include thoughts about time too. Now it will be said that this still leaves acts of thinking. Surely, it will be said, such acts must take place in time. Very well, let us see what is involved in such acts. Someone asks me what I am doing, and I reply: 'Thinking'. What might this mean? Ostensibly it means that I am going through a series of mental operations; trying to find a way out of an awkward dilemma, say, pondering over the book I have just read, recollecting some past experience, planning my next chess move, grappling with some deep philosophical puzzle, or whatever. All this takes time. I 'experience' the mental process I happen to be engaged in as an ongoing event, and my reply, accordingly, is phrased in the continuous present. Looking back, I might make this more explicit by saying, for example, 'It took me a heck of a long time to sort out that problem', or 'I was mulling it over in my head for a long time before I finally managed to get on top of it', etc. The point is that I represent such phenomena to myself as occupying portions of my biographical time, and this fact obviously is of crucial importance in determining how I shall behave and what I shall do in any given circumstances. For example, just now I am engaged in trying to discover the reason why my computer does not function as it should. There was a sudden hitch a moment ago when in response to some fairly simple commands a series of error messages appeared on the screen. I am anxious to get on with the task in hand and am already growing nervous and quite flustered as a result of my repeated failure to identify the cause of the trouble. The consciousness of time passing weighs heavily upon me as the realization grows that I won't be able to accomplish what I had set out to do as speedily as I had hoped. The acute sense of the 'loss' of time is directly responsible for fashioning my present mood and my attitude to my work.

All this is trivially true. Yet what does it actually prove? To begin with, there is a distinction to be made between the thought of time passing and time passing. My actions, it should be noted, are prompted by the thought of time passing; but that I have a thought of time passing is no proof that time is passing in actual fact. I represent my experiences to myself in a temporal fashion. Indeed, my verbal accounts of them are replete with tensed verbs and indexical temporal adverbs. By why should this necessarily be an indication of anything going on in real time? That I think of certain phenomena in temporal terms hardly amounts to evidence that such phenomena are temporal *simpliciter*. The fact that they are conceived of by me as occurring within the framework of 'indexical time' proves nothing about their temporality *per se*.

In sum, the sceptical argument reduces to the following two propositions: first, that objective thought-contents, including thoughts about time, are not themselves temporal; and, secondly, that thinking, or acts of thought, while represented by ourselves as temporal phenomena, need not necessarily be indicative of the existence of any actual temporal processes. I posit myself as the subject of successive acts of thought, but whether such acts occur in real time is yet to be shown. It is by no means certain beyond all doubt that I change my attributes in real time, as distinct from merely 'projecting' myself as changing.

7

THE REALITY OF CHANGE

WHAT reply should we give to the sceptic? The key issue that emerges from our discussion in the preceding chapter seems to be one of the interpretation of 'indexical' time; in particular, what inferences, if any, regarding real time and real change can be drawn from the distinctions of tense? The sceptic is likely to approve wholeheartedly of our criticism of naturalism. He might even go as far as accepting not just that indexical temporal notions are centrally involved in the way we explain ourselves to ourselves, but, moreover, that their availability is an essential pre-condition of the intelligibility of change in general. But this is about as far as he is likely to go. His position remains that no propositions that depend for their intelligibility upon indexical temporal notions, and hence none of what might be called 'irreducibly tensed' propositions, need ever be true; and therefore that no affirmative inferences are warranted regarding the reality of time or objective change. He is trying to undermine any such inferences by, in effect, inviting us to contemplate the possibility of a self which, though conceiving of itself and its own activities under the aspect of time, nevertheless remains extra-temporal in essence.

In point of fact, this is precisely where his argument comes to grief. For, as we shall see, whereas the idea of an extra-temporal self pure and simple, vacuous though it probably is, does not seem to be logically contradictory, the idea of a self that explains itself to itself in temporal terms while (metaphysically) remaining outside time is quite obviously incoherent. The self does not merely 'think' itself as temporally extended; it is temporally extended, and structurally entails the existence of objective change.

Memory: A Second Look

The argument against the sceptic will be mounted in two stages. First, we shall have to comment on the centrality of the notion of indexical time, in particular by highlighting the dependence upon it of one of the fundamental distinctions in terms of which we talk about the phenomena of change, namely, the distinction between numerical and qualitative identity. Then, after setting out some ideas for a structuralist treatment of change, we shall show why propositions that contain, or presuppose as a condition of their own intelligibility, indexical temporal notions, cannot be uniformly false.

But before we launch into the argument proper, it is necessary to dispose of the view that there is a relatively easy short cut to victory over the sceptic via a conceptual analysis of memory claims. In the preceding chapter we have already commented on memory claims, in particular with regard to the question of objectivity. However, it might be objected that too much emphasis was placed on objectivity and far too little on truth. Surely, it might be said, memory claims not only have to satisfy certain objectivity conditions: they also have to be sometimes true. Not just potentially true, but true as a matter of fact. For suppose they were always false. Then there could be no intelligible concept of memory. Since nothing happened before now, there would be nothing to remember. We could not even distinguish intelligibly between what we *think* is happening now and what we *think* happened in the past. One can coherently think that x occurred in the past, only if it is in principle possible that x occurred in the past, but such a possibility is excluded *ex hypothesi*. Consequently, there can be no significant concept of apparent, let alone, genuine memory. If my memory cannot be correct, it cannot be incorrect either. If the past is unreal, we cannot even significantly pretend there is one.[1]

What strikes one first about this argument is that it is circular without being in any way illuminating. (Not all circularity in

[1] An argument along the above lines can be found in N. Malcolm, 'Memory and the Past', in *Knowledge and Certainty* (Englewood Cliffs, NJ, 1963), 187.

philosophical reasoning need necessarily be vacuous or vicious.) The thesis that is being advanced is that the existence of the past is presupposed by the distinction between correct and incorrect memory, and the latter distinction in turn is explained by postulating the existence of the past. But quite apart from this, the argument, if closely inspected, can be seen to derive from a basic misunderstanding of the sceptical position. What the sceptic is saying, of course, is not that memory claims are necessarily false, only that they might be false as a matter of fact. It is conceivable that some memory claims might be true, but it is equally conceivable that none are, and this is all that the sceptic needs for his purposes. Notice that if no memory claims happen to be true, this does not render the distinction between correct and incorrect memory unintelligible. It is only if no such claims could be true as a matter of logical necessity that the distinction between correct and incorrect memory ceases to have any meaning.

In short, the sceptic is disputing that the distinction between correct and incorrect memory logically entails the reality of the past, and hence he is rejecting the very premiss upon which the above anti-sceptical argument is hinged.

Why is the Notion of Indexical Time Necessary?

Clearly a different approach is needed in order to meet the sceptical challenge. The sceptic's contention is that the possession of the notion of indexical time, and hence of the distinctions of tense, affords no evidence of the existence of real time or objective change. Nevertheless, the fact remains that the notion of indexical time is profoundly implicated in a whole array of concepts and ideas in terms of which we make sense of the world around us, and, as a first move in what, it is hoped, will be a more effective anti-sceptical argument, we shall have to take a closer look at how this affects one categorial distinction in particular, namely, that between numerical and qualitative identity.

As scarcely needs emphasizing, Tweedledum and Tweedledee alike though they be, Tweedledum and Tweedledee are two for all to see. We take it as a matter of course that there can be qualitatively completely identical things that are, nevertheless, numerically distinguishable. In other words, no single thing, we normally assume, is individuated solely by the qualities— or, phrased in the idiom of attributes, by the attributes—it has at any given time. This assumption is fundamental to our grasp of change, for if any qualitative alteration entailed a change of numerical identity, there would be nothing of which change could intelligibly be predicated.[2]

This seems obvious enough. Change (I am here deliberately excluding existential change, which will be discussed later) involves an acquisition of incompatible attributes over time. This demands that the subject of change remain numerically the same from one moment in time to the next (with the emphasis very much upon 'numerically'). If the identity of the subject of change consisted exclusively in the kind of attributes it had at any given time, then strictly there would be no change (as defined above), for any acquisition of a new attribute, including such a thing as a simple mechanical displacement from one location to another, would merely signal the presence of a new object, however small and imperceptible the resulting difference, or differences, might be. There would be no justification for supposing that anything endures through time as a specimen rather than a species, and consequently no grounds for ascribing change to anything at all.

This granted, the immediate question is, where does the idea of numerical as distinct from qualitative identity come from? What makes this distinction intelligible? And how, in particular, are the *criteria* of numerical differentiation to be defined? In ordinary circumstances we generally find it sufficient to point to the spatial location, or place. But, as was shown earlier,

---

[2] Those philosophers who regard the so-called 'principle of the identity of indiscernibles', according to which two things that coincide in all their attributes are numerically indistinguishable, as a sufficient principle of individuation, either have to forgo the distinction between numerical and qualitative identity (and hence the possibility of accounting for change) or else they have to assume that there are attributes, which, unlike qualities, are not sharable, even in principle, by different individuals, and then the question arises what such individuating attributes might be. I shall argue that spatial attributes, on their own, cannot fulfil this role.

adequate though this may be for practical purposes, it is not satisfactory at a deeper level, for it merely raises the problem of individuation of places. In addition, the spatial criterion, even within the limited context within which it may be said to work, is crucially dependent upon the considerations of time. Thus if two qualitatively identical individuals are to be numerically distinguishable, then evidently it is only provided they can occupy two different positions in space *at the same time*. In other words, numerical differentiation via spatial location, at the very least presupposes, and depends upon, the intelligibility of temporal designations such as 'at the same time' and 'at a different time', and upon the possibility of differentiating time from space.

Now conceivably it might be objected that all this really is much ado about nothing. Surely any difficulties concerning individuation, it might be said, can easily be avoided by abandoning identity in favour of similarity, and by interpreting material particulars, for example, as constructions out of certain similar, or near-similar, basic elements. There is no need, in order to account for change, to postulate the existence of any numerically identical continuants. The phenomenon of change consists precisely in the fact that there is nothing that literally survives unaltered for any length of time. It is not just conceivable but very probable that the world is made up entirely of fluctuating agglomerations of essentially fleeting basic constituents.

This approach (notably favoured by the phenomenalists) does not solve the problem, however; it merely shifts it on to the basic constituents, whatever such constituents might be. For the questions that instantly crop up are: What are the *individuative features* of such constituents? and: Are such constituents individuated solely by their qualities, or should we think of them as being distinguishable from each other numerically as well as qualitatively? If they can differ from each other *solo numero* and not just qualitatively, then again we are faced with the problem of accounting for numerical identity through time. If, on the other hand, they are individuated exclusively by their qualities, then there is no change, and no accretion of such constituents can add up to one, if only because the spatio-temporal region where such accretion might take place cannot be identified independently of such constituents; and it is not clear what else conceivably might act as an enduring peg to hold such constituents together. So the attempt to solve the problem by replacing identity with similarity fails.

If, however, we need the concept of numerical, and not just that of qualitative, identity, in order to be able to account for the possibility of change, then, it seems, a fundamental requirement is that we should be able to differentiate time from space. For if time were inseparable from space; if, for example, the time co-ordinate were to be conceived of as just another component of a homogeneous four-dimensional structure such as so-called Euclidean space–time, then, strictly, no clear meaning could be attached to the claim that objects within such a structure endure as numerically, rather than qualitatively, the same, for any alteration of space–time features would in effect bring about a change of identity, and, in consequence, one could no longer significantly talk about change. Numerical identity would in effect collapse into qualitative identity.

It follows that if there is to be real change, there must be a possibility of differentiating time from space. An object's survival as an existentially unique particular depends upon its ability to weather a change of attributes, *including* the change of its spatial attributes. Spatial position on its own, strictly, is not individuative of anything. As we saw earlier, the 'spatial criterion' of numerical differentiation of necessity involves an appeal to temporal notions. If a particular is individuated by the place it occupies, then it is only provided that all the particulars there are at any given time simultaneously occupy different places relative to each other; and, of course, this only prompts the question, 'What is meant by "different places"?' As it turns out, even an appeal to the simultaneous occupation of different places is not going to be quite enough to enable us to account for the sort of particular identity that is necessary to explain the possibility of change; for what is needed is the numerical identity not just *at* an instant, but over a number of successive time instants. It is only provided the object remains numerically the same sufficiently long to acquire different, indeed incompatible attributes, that we can significantly speak of it as 'changing'.

So the upshot of the whole matter is this: that change demands as a condition of its intelligibility a distinction between numerical and qualitative identity, and the latter distinction, in turn, presupposes the possibility of a differentiation of time from space. An object maintains its numerical identity, and hence its existential uniqueness, not simply in virtue of occupying a particular position in space, but in virtue of surviving a change of its spatial predicates; or, to put it differently, it does so inasmuch as the value of its time curve remains unaffected by any alteration of its spatial co-ordinates; the implication of this being that it is time rather than space that holds the key to numerical identity.

And therein lies the moral of the whole story. For time in so far as it is differentiated from space is just the indexical time of past, present, and future. Its source is the self that portrays itself to itself as biographically enduring, while at the same time projecting this feature of temporal persistence into an objective realm.

A Structuralist Approach to Change

Indexical time is thus a vital prerequisite of the intelligibility of change. Change as an acquisition of incompatible attributes over time demands the idea of an enduring and existentially unique ontological particular, and access to the latter idea is gained by way of the notion of indexical time.

Nevertheless, this account of the matter, though accurate, does not convey the full picture, for on closer examination it turns out that what we have here is a logical structure of several closely interrelated and interlocking ideas. The view advanced above, namely that indexical time as a principle of distinction between numerical and qualitative identity represents a source of the categorial apparatus in terms of which we describe the phenomena of attributive change, if taken in isolation, suggests that the self portrays the world the way it does because it conceives of itself the way it does. In fact, there are equally cogent reasons for claiming that the self would be unable coherently to think of itself as biographically extended, and

hence as subject to temporal change, *unless* it pictured the world
the way it does; that is, the distinction between numerical and
qualitative identity, together with its cognate concepts and
categories, especially as applied to external material particulars,
is an essential constituent of the structure of ideas upon which
the temporal self must rely in order to have a clear grasp of its
own nature.

More specifically, what I wish to contend is this: that there
exist close structural ties between (1) the notion of a biographically extended self (indeed the notion of a plurality of such
selves), (2) the distinction between numerical and qualitative
identity, (3) the idea of enduring material particulars (the
material continuants), and (4) the possibility of attributive
change; in other words, that all these ideas are mutually
complementary and interdependent.

In what follows, I shall sketch out an underpinning argument
for the above thesis, drawing freely on the results of my
discussions so far.

Consider, first, the concept of a material particular in the light
of what has been said about numerical and qualitative identity.
I am now sitting at my desk on what is a fairly comfortable
chair. It is the same chair that I was sitting on yesterday, and
also the day before yesterday. The particular I am referring to is
not just an identical subject of different attributes: it is an
enduring, and hence in principle reidentifiable subject of
different, indeed successively altering attributes. Now, the idea
of such a particular presupposes, and is unintelligible without,
the idea of a temporally enduring self. The self that conceives of
itself as biographically extended in unidirectional time yields
us the distinction between numerical and qualitative identity,
and the latter distinction in turn underlies the concept of a
reidentifiable material particular. But, as can be easily seen, the
converse also holds; that is, the self needs the idea of a
reidentifiable material particular in order to be able to make
clear sense of what is involved in the notion of its own
temporality. The reason for this is quite simple. If there were no
reidentifiable material particulars, there would be no reference
points in relation to which the self, through an act of
reidentification, would be able to make manifest its own

persistence through time. The self needs the idea of reidentifiable external particulars, if only to know the difference between thinking oneself as enduring, and enduring in real time. We said earlier that the self has a notion of its own extendedness in time by virtue of having a notion of its own past. But the point that needs to be emphasized is that the notion that the self has of its own past acquires an objective reference only via the idea of enduring, and hence in principle reidentifiable, external items. If no significant references could be made to such items, if no such references could conceivably be true, then my claim that I persist through time as numerically identical would be rendered vacuous. Without the notion of a numerically re-identifiable external particular, the distinction of numerical and qualitative identity would cease to have any discernible meaning. The self would no longer be in a position to distinguish between the same specimen and a different specimen of the same species, and would forfeit the sense of its own existential uniqueness. And this only goes to show that the idea of a numerically identical self and that of a numerically identical 'external' particular belong closely together; in other words, if it is true that there can be no reidentifiable external particulars without temporally extended selves, it is also true that there can be no temporally extended selves without reidentifiable external particulars.

Let us now broaden the basis of the argument by introducing the idea of objective order. Part of the conception that the self has of itself as temporally extended in unidirectional time, we said earlier, is the idea of an unalterable past, and hence the idea of an order that cannot be arbitrarily changed. Acts of recollection by their very nature presuppose the idea of such an order. But so do acts of *anticipation*. I have just picked up what I take to be a pen—it has the familiar slim, tubular body, painted orange—and I expect it to leave a trace on paper as I scribble a note with it, holding it between my thumb and my forefinger. It might do so, or possibly it might not. It may turn out that what I picked up was not a pen at all; or, if it was a pen, that it had run out of ink or was damaged in some way. My anticipations might or might not prove to be correct, and the circumstance that I could be mistaken points to an order that is grounded in the object and is independent of the order of my experiences, or my desires.

But evidently here too the logical traffic flows in both directions. Thus it is not merely the self's notion of itself as temporally extended in unidirectional time, and with it the idea of correct and incorrect recollections and anticipations, that give us the grasp of the idea of an objective order independent of our desires, but, conversely too, we need the idea of such an order if we are to have a clear notion of potentially correct or incorrect recollections and anticipations, and generally of ourselves as extended in unidirectional time. For how else could the distinction between correct and incorrect be explained? If there is no order that may deviate from how I conceive of it on any given occasion, then I can never be mistaken, and the concept of error becomes meaningless. In other words, if it is true that the idea of an objective order presupposes the idea of error, it is equally true that the latter idea presupposes the former: neither is intelligible without the other. Moreover, given the errors of anticipation as well as those of recollection, we need the idea of an order based in the object and not just derived from the notion of one's own unalterable past.

Finally, consider the link between the idea of an objective order and that of a plurality of selves, in particular bearing in mind what was said earlier about objective validity. Part of the notion of self as extended in unidirectional time, I have argued, is the possibility of correct and incorrect recollections and anticipations, and hence the distinction between what seems to me to be the case on any given occasion and what is actually the case, and with it the idea of an objective as distinct from a merely subjective order. But any claims about what actually is the case can be correct or incorrect only under certain conditions, that is, only provided they satisfy certain criteria in virtue of which they qualify as valid truth candidates; and such criteria, as was shown earlier, necessarily involve a reference to a social context.

Now it is not difficult to see that here the exactly similar situation obtains as in the two previous cases, i.e. the argument cuts both ways. Thus manifestly without the idea of the criteria of coherence and appropriateness, and by inference without the idea of a social context, there can be no clear distinction between what I myself, for any reason, may regard as meaningful on a given occasion, and what is objectively meaningful, and consequently no clear notion of the distinction between what can and cannot be significantly claimed to be true. Of course, we already do have some notion of an objective order from our notion of the past, and what is more—in connection, especially, with the 'errors of anticipation'—we have the general idea of an order grounded in the object. Yet this inevitably would remain a hazy concept without the idea of the criteria whereby a decision might be made between what can and what cannot be significantly asserted about such an order, that is, without the criteria of *objective validity*.

So the general inference that suggests itself is that the idea of reidentifiable material particulars and the idea of a plurality of selves both necessarily enter into the concept of the self as temporally extended in unidirectional time, and, moreover, that each of these ideas is semantically implicated in all three. From here conceptual links branch out in a number of different directions. The above discussion provides just a glimpse of some of the key features of what is clearly a complex network of ideas that criss-cross and intertwine, and derive what meaning they have from their respective positions within the network, which acts as their common pool of significance. However, there is no need, at this point, to pursue these logical links in their intricate detail. What is of interest in the present context, and needs to be specially emphasized, is that the notion of a temporally extended self that did not presuppose the idea of a world that included reidentifiable material particulars and other selves, and, conversely, the idea of a world that included reidentifiable material particulars but was logically independent of the existence of selves, must both be rejected as incoherent.

A further result that needs to be highlighted is that the idea of a self as temporally extended in real time demands as a condition of own meaningfulness the idea of *altering* as well as enduring external particulars, for it is only via a reference to such particulars that a clear distinction can be drawn between the mere thought of one being temporally extended and being temporally extended in actual fact.

Is it Possible that All Tensed Propositions might be False?

Let us now move on to stage two of our argument. What has been established so far, namely that the idea of a temporal self and the idea of objective change are logically interlinked, is not likely to satisfy the recalcitrant sceptic. For he is likely to point out that important though this result might be, what needs to be proved is not just that there exist close structural ties between certain ideas, but whether anything corresponding to such ideas exists in *reality*.

Consider memory again. The meaningfulness of a memory claim, I have argued, has to do with certain objectivity conditions in virtue of which the claim in question qualifies as a valid truth candidate. Such objectivity conditions involve a series of assumptions, in particular the unidirectional flow of time from past to future and the possibility of other selves. But the point that the sceptic is making, of course, is that even if memory claims can be regarded as meaningful in the light of such conditions, they *need never be true*.

More generally, if it is accepted, as my discussion so far suggests it should be, that tensed propositions are needed to describe the phenomena of change, the sceptic's position reduces to the thesis that, as a matter of fact, *all* tensed propositions might be false; and it is clear that there is no prospect of overthrowing his argument from a naturalistic point of view. What is more, on naturalistic premises, not even a moderately satisfactory account can be provided of the conditions under which tensed propositions make sense. This indeed was one of the implications of Zeno's arguments. (I should reiterate yet again that by 'naturalism' I mean the view that all the facts there are can be expressed in impersonal, or third-person, terms, without recourse to indexical expressions whose meaning depends upon the conditions of their utterance.) In short, there can be no viable naturalistic theory of change.

What we now find is that a structural analysis of the concept of temporal self does not necessarily help root out any residual doubts about the reality of change either. What it does, it seems, is merely enable us to clarify the conditions under which propositions descriptive of change can be *understood*. The sceptic is a veteran of many battles and does not give up the fight lightly, even though, for tactical reasons, he may decide to withdraw from some of his more exposed outposts. Thus conceivably he might concede that our analysis does indeed show that the idea of change, and hence of becoming in general, is embedded in the notion of the self, and, moreover, that this represents an advance as compared with the naturalistic approach. Nevertheless, he is at the same time likely to insist that in merely providing an account of how change is possible nothing has been proved about its actual occurrence. The fact, if it is fact, that the notion of a temporally extended self plays a key role in any elucidation of the *concept* of change does not show either that reality is changing or that the self itself is necessarily temporal.

Does this mean that despite all our efforts the sceptic can yet hold his ground, and survive the assault essentially unscathed? No, it certainly does not, as will become apparent presently.

Crucial to the success of the sceptical argument is the supposition that the self whilst conceiving of itself as temporally extended might, nevertheless, be atemporal in essence, and this supposition cannot be coherently entertained. To begin with, given that I cannot know myself except under the aspect of time, then, if I am indeed atemporal in essence, it follows that I cannot know myself as I 'really' am, or even if in referring to my supposed atemporal essence I am referring to the same self. But, then, what meaning might be attached to the hypothesis of my 'essential' atemporality? The only reply that could be given to this, it seems, is that the notion of an extra-temporal self is not logically contradictory. But this is a lame reply, for if it is in principle impossible to have any knowledge of such a self, then, even assuming that the notion is not contradictory, it is surely vacuous, unless it can be vindicated on other grounds. Besides, we are concerned here not just with the notion of an extra-temporal self, but with the notion of an extra-temporal self that at the same time conceives of itself under the aspect of time, and it is easy to see that the latter notion does give rise to contradictions. If an extra-temporal self is possible, it cannot— logically cannot—be identical in essence with 'our' kind of self.

The simple point is that if the conception that I have of my own selfhood depends upon the idea that I have of myself as extended in unidirectional time, then I can not at the same time consistently think of myself as extra-temporal in essence. The self does not endure as an extra-temporal substance; rather it survives by constituting itself as a unity of biographical time, in particular through successive acts of 'appropriation' of experiences. In some way it is like the operation of counting, whereby each of the successive number utterances—their physical disconnectedness notwithstanding—conveys the desired message inasmuch as it involves a reference to the previous members of the series of which itself forms part.

Transposed into familiar theological terms, the hypothesis that I am essentially extra-temporal is another way of saying that my selfhood is anchored in an eternal (or, more accurately, 'atemporal') soul. But if the above argument is anything to go by, the self is neither a simulacrum of the soul, nor is it substantivally identical with it.[3] One extreme possibility that the sceptic seems to be wishing us to consider is that of a self engaged in an elaborate *pretence* of temporality. But this can hardly be taken seriously. Given the usual meaning of 'pretending', to pretend to do x means to strike a posture or engage in behaviour intended to elicit the impression that one is doing something other than what one is doing in actual fact. It is a deliberate act of dissimulation, and the *awareness* of the pretence on the part of the agent is an integral part of the act. But if the self cannot know itself other than under the aspect of time, then there cannot be any pretending on its part of acting in time either. In other words, the idea is amusing but ridiculous.

The same applies to yet another notion that conceivably might be put forward, namely that the self is unwittingly deceiving itself in supposing it is extended in time. For even on the assumption that the deception is unwitting, the self must be capable—in principle, at least, if not in actual fact—of discovering the identity of the deceiver, and the circumstance that

---

[3] If souls qualify as selves they cannot be 'our' kind of self, if only because, being extra-temporal, they lack the source from which we derive our conception of numerical identity, and hence the sense of our own existential uniqueness.

the deception had taken place; and, of course, this is precisely what it is logically debarred from doing. It cannot detect the deception, not even in principle. But, then, to all intents and purposes there is none.

The Problem of Existential Change

And there we have to rest our case. Nevertheless there are other issues that still need to be resolved. The mere fact that change is a necessary feature of a world that includes selves does not explain why change should occur at all. Nor does it provide any clues to how the problem of existential change should be addressed. In my discussions so far, I have concerned myself principally with the conditions of the possibility of alteration, or attributive change; and the general conclusion that has emerged from these discussions is that a naturalistic treatment of attributive change leads to a conceptual cul-de-sac, and has to be replaced with a structuralist approach if the possibility of objective change is to be made intelligible. But the question still remains: How does existential change fit into this picture? Can the phenomena of a thing's coming into being or going out of existence be characterized as genuine cases of change, and in what sense?

Existential change, as we saw, was a focal point of controversy in traditional metaphysics, giving rise to a number of different and often conflicting theories. In general, such theories involved a deployment of one of the two principal rival reductivist strategies. One such strategy consisted in looking for a suitable (usually naturalistically conceived) ontological model within which the phenomenon of existential change could be shown to be ultimately reducible to that of the attributive sort. The other strategy involved pursuing the opposite route, and attempting to show that all forms of change, in the final analysis, reduced to existential change, and hence that the whole concept of change could be shown to be at root contradictory.

Neither strategy worked. The former strategy was traditionally deployed by metaphysical monists and metaphysical pluralists alike, and was largely carried over into natural science. But, as was shown in Chapter 3, this approach to the problem, so far from achieving its objective, merely generated a conceptual confusion and afforded no protection against the depredations of scepticism. The main source of difficulty was that, although the strategy in question was built around the distinction between numerical and qualitative identity, given the naturalistic bias of the whole enterprise, no clear account could be provided of the conditions that made this distinction possible, let alone necessary, with the result that the concept of change remained obscure.

The monists in particular sought to solve the puzzle of existential change by postulating an eternal universal substance, of which all forms of change were supposed to be predicable. However, there was no indication as to what such a substance might be independently of its multifarious phenomenal manifestations, or how it could alter its state without forfeiting its own identity. The pluralist approach, by contrast, involved interpreting change, including the coming into being and demise of objects of experience, in terms of a process of clustering and realignment of a plurality of basic elements of one sort or another. But this did not hold out much promise of a solution to the problem either. For if such basic elements—or basic constituents of reality—are distinguished from each other numerically as well as qualitatively, then the question that needs to be answered is, just what does their numerical as distinct from their qualitative identity consist in? If, on the other hand, they are distinguished from each other solely by their qualities, then ultimately there can be no change.

In short, the central issue was one of how the basic substance or substances (or whatever the basic constituents of reality happen to be) could acquire contradictory predicates that are consistent with change, while at the same time enduring unaltered for any length of time; that is, how could change be squared up with identity?

Now at first glance, it might seem that a key to the solution to this puzzle lies in the distinction between essential and inessential qualities. Surely, it might be said, the subject of change, as long as it endures, maintains its identity in respect of its essential qualities, and alters in respect of its inessential qualities. Yet this is no solution, for the central question still remains unanswered, namely, what holds the essential qualities together? If the identity of the subject consists literally in what is termed its 'essential qualities', then the subject is a universal, and hence, strictly, is not subject to alteration. If, on the other hand, the subject is defined in terms of the totality of its qualities at any given time, then any change of qualities of whatever sort entails a change of the subject, and again there can be no change, for if a given x 'changed' it would literally become other than what it is, and manifestly nothing can become 'other than what it is'.

In point of fact, this seems to me to have been the general underlying theme of the Eleatics' critical reasoning.[4] What their

---

[4] This is how I understand Zeno's 'paradox of likeness' from Plato's *Parmenides*. Ostensibly Zeno's paradox is aimed against pluralism. But, as I have already emphasized, Zeno's arguments against pluralism are inseparable from his critique of change. The main point that Zeno was trying to put across, it seems to me, was this. In order to provide a rational account of change it is necessary to explain the possibility of reconciling two conflicting ideas: the idea of the 'oneness' of the subject of change with the idea of a plurality of its attributes. Talk of change involves the assumption that the subject of change can acquire new, indeed incompatible, attributes, or 'characters', without forfeiting its own identity. But on naturalistic premises, at any rate, this is impossible. A thing that changed would be both 'like' and 'unlike' itself. It would be 'like itself' in so far as it functioned as the same subject of change, and yet it would no longer be 'like itself' inasmuch as its attributes would have altered. Hence change is impossible. Evidence supporting such an interpretation can be found in Melissus, who appears to use 'like' (ὅμοιον) in the sense of 'the same in character at all times', and 'unchanging' (see F. M. Cornford, *Plato and Parmenides* (London, 1969), 68). Melissus also appears to confirm that the Eleatics tried to expose the contradictions in the idea of change by deliberately interpreting all change as existential change: 'If what is is changed, it cannot be alike, but what was before must perish, and what was not must come to be. If, then, it should become different by a hair in ten thousand years, in all time it will all perish' (frag. 7, trans. Cornford. I should emphasize that the interpretation of the fragment is my own not Cornford's). As for the 'paradox of likeness', the efforts of Plato's Socrates (in the *Parmenides*) to resolve the paradox by appealing to the idea of 'participation' hardly amounted to a plausible argument. The gist of Socrates' criticism was that Zeno had failed to distinguish between contradictory characters, on the one hand, and the thing qualified by contradictory characters, on the other. The circumstance that there are contradictory or mutually incompatible characters, Socrates argued, did not preclude the possibility of the same thing *having* incompatible characters, viz. by 'partaking'—as it altered—in the relevant Ideas. But leaving the specific difficulties of the platonist concept of participation to one side, this 'solution' presupposed that the idea of a numerically enduring particular capable of

arguments amounted to was that the attributive model of change urged upon us by ordinary common sense and its philosophical offspring, the metaphysics of things and attributes (in all its many guises), ought not to be taken on trust, but should have its credentials carefully examined. For what assurance was there that this model reflected the structure of the actual world? What was the justification for assuming its objective validity? The unquestioning application of such a model in a naturalistic context, so far from helping to throw light on the possibility of change, merely generated more bafflement about the whole issue, with the concept of a subject of change in particular remaining clouded in mystery. As a result, the only alternative seemed to be to interpret all change as existential change, with the consequent denial of the possibility of change altogether.

Change and Selves

The Eleatics embraced that alternative unflinchingly. But the resolution of the problem, as I have urged, lies not in an Eleatic type of reductivism, but in a reinterpretation of the attributive model, involving a recognition of its limitations within the context of the 'conditions that make its application *meaningful*. More precisely, it lies in an abandonment of the naturalistic ontology in favour of what I have called a 'structuralist' approach to the phenomenon of change. And, as we saw, this requires, in the first instance, that selves be brought into the picture.

The position that I have advanced in particular with regard to selves may be briefly summed up as follows. First, change is unintelligible without the distinction between numerical and qualitative identity, and the latter distinction cannot be made clear without a reference to selves. The idea of an ontological item acquiring incompatible attributes over time and surviving

successively acquiring incompatible characters (and with it the distinction between numerical and qualitative identity) was well understood and required no explanatory comment, whereas the whole point of Zeno's argument, as I see it, was that this idea stood in dire need of elucidation.

as an identical subject of change presupposes, and is inseparable from, the notion of self. Moreover, these two ideas are logically interdependent. Secondly, the existence of an objectively changing world demands not just the possibility but the actual existence of selves. If there are no selves, there is no change. Furthermore, the supposition of the existence of selves in the plural is part of the conditions that make the very concept of self intelligible. Thirdly, and directly following from the preceding two points, no description of the world is complete that does not include the linguistic instruments of self-reference; in other words, there is no complete description of the world without indexicals.

What thus emerges is a picture of a close logical relationship between objective change and temporally extended selves. It is a very different world from the one painted by naturalistic reductivism. Naturalistic metaphysics, as a rule, has a great deal to say about entities as subjects of predication, but very little about the conditions under which a subject of predication qualifies as a subject of change. It is principally preoccupied with the problem of deciding which subjects of predication do, and which do not, qualify as basic, on the assumption that the basic subjects of predication coincide with the basic existents. But change is not a phenomenon that is confined, or can be reduced to the properties of such existents. Any number of different things can act as subjects of change: from chairs and tables to football clubs and universities; and even events, as we saw, in certain circumstances can perform that role. When we posit an item as a subject of change, we posit it as a numerically enduring particular within a specific context, and, again contextually, allow for the possibility of its perishing, or surviving a change of attributes—in some cases surviving even a catastrophic change of attributes without necessarily forfeiting its numerical identity. All this presupposes, and is unintelligible without, a reference to selves.

Consider again one of our earlier examples, namely the sofa converted into a bed, and vice versa. Evidently, although the sofa *qua* sofa literally cannot acquire the properties of a bed, the particular which is contextually identified as sofa-like *can* become bed-like; in other words, the sofa-shaped thing does have the capacity of shedding the sofa properties and acquiring bed-like features. This is consonant with, and a consequence of, the distinction between numerical and qualitative identity. In positing a given object as a numerically enduring particular that is characterized by certain attributes, we are by implication allowing the possibility of that object suffering a change of attributes without ceasing to be the same. This, it should be emphasized, does not mean that, in the final analysis, the subject of change in such a case can only be some undefined substance that underlies, and is independent of, any qualifying attributes, a bare particular stripped of all its qualities, and existing in a cognitively inaccessible realm, like some sort of 'thing in itself'. What actually exists are determinate individuals, not bare particulars. Nevertheless, we can make sense of change only by distinguishing between the numerical and the qualitative aspect of such individuals. Normally what happens is that such an individual is contextually assigned the function of a numerically identical subject of change. In our example, the 'sofa-thing' fulfils that function not just when the sofa gets scratched or coffee-stained, but also when the sofa is turned into a bed; and the 'bed-thing' is assigned the same role when the operation is reversed.

Moreover, what applies to inanimate things applies also to living beings.[5] Thus although the caterpillar *qua* caterpillar can never be a butterfly, caterpillars nevertheless *do* become

[5] This, incidentally, highlights a difficulty that afflicts Aristotle's concept of matter. Matter, in his definition (*Metaph.* 1042ᵃ), is that which is (only) potentially a 'this', i.e. determinate individual. At the same time, it is seen as something that persists, or endures, through a change of attributes. But given that matter as such has no form, the question is, in what sense exactly can it be said to remain 'the same'? Aristotle seems to think that matter must at least be 'countable'. But it is not altogether clear just what is being 'counted' in such a case. Evidently, if the matter is to stay the same, then, being formless, i.e. without qualities, it can do so only in some purely numerical sense. However, Aristotle seems unable to throw any light on the concept of numerical, as distinct from qualitative, identity. Some commentators have tried to solve this problem by interpreting matter in terms of quantity, and claiming, accordingly, that what persists through attributive change is just quantity. (Cf. K. C. Cook, *Aristotle on Matter and Coming to Be* (Ann Arbor, Mich., 1980). But while this may work in the case of a lump of bronze that is made into a statue, or even in the case of the bed and the sofa—the quantity of the matter in both cases remaining the same—it clearly does not help to explain the numerical identity of a growing as well as altering living organism.

butterflies. Here, as in other cases, we can make sense of what goes on only by logically dismantling, as it were, the object in question into its numerical and its qualitative facets, and positing, accordingly, a caterpillar-like numerically identical particular as an enduring peg for a series of attributes. But it should be noted that this dismantling occurs within the context of the self's own cognitive activity. There are no numerically enduring, existentially unique particulars independently of such an activity; nor is there change independently of such an activity—even though (as was shown earlier) the self at the same time requires the supposition of external, numerically enduring particulars in order to have a clear grasp of itself as extended in time. As to the question of what ought to be treated as such a particular in what circumstances, and for how long, in the final analysis this can only be settled within the general framework of our own interests and needs.

It follows that in most cases we can get round the problem of existential change by positing a numerically enduring particular that *contextually* carries the burden of a catastrophic change of attributes. But, of course, this does not help sort out the problem of the self's own existential change—its own coming into and going out of existence. The situation in such a case is evidently different. Thus when one self perishes or comes into being, there is not another self of which these events might be predicated. No account in terms of the attributive model can work here. And that is just about all that can be said about the matter. Selves are neither substances nor attributes of substances. The only way to characterize them, perhaps, is as focal points within the broad range of the cognitive activity that is integral to the world's own structure, and, in a sense, helps sustain the latter in being. When an individual self emerges into existence, a type of cognitive activity particularizes itself in a physical setting, and its going out of existence signifies the disappearance of such an activity from such a setting. Nevertheless, selves are not simply gratuitous or isolated cognitive happenings. Rather, they seem to be episodic constituents of a global event, glimmering and fading like specks of light on the rippled surface of the water as the breeze sweeps across the horizon.

SELECT BIBLIOGRAPHY

ARISTOTLE, *On Generation and Corruption*, trans. H. H. Joachim, in *The Complete Works of Aristotle*, i, ed. J. Barnes (Princeton University Press: Princeton, NJ, 1984). See also *De Generatione et Corruptione*, trans. C. J. F. Williams (Clarendon Press: Oxford, 1982).

—— *Metaphysics*, trans. W. D. Ross, in *The Complete Works of Aristotle*, ii, ed. J. Barnes (Princeton University Press: Princeton, NJ, 1984).

—— *Physics*, trans. R. P. Hardie and R. K. Gaye, in *The Complete Works of Aristotle*, i, ed. J. Barnes (Princeton University Press: Princeton, NJ, 1984).

AVERROES, *On Aristotle's* De Generatione et Corruptione, trans. S. Kurland (Mediaeval Academy of America: Cambridge, Mass., 1958).

BARNES, J., *The Presocratic Philosophers*, 2 vols. (Routledge and Kegan Paul: London, 1979).

CHAPPEL, J. F., 'Whitehead's Theory of Becoming', *Journal of Philosophy*, 58 (1961), 516–28.

COOK, K. C., *Aristotle on Matter and Coming to Be* (University Microfilm: Ann Arbor, Mich., and London, 1980).

CORNFORD, F. M., *Plato and Parmenides* (Routledge and Kegan Paul: London, 1969).

DAVIDSON, D., *Essays on Actions and Events* (Clarendon Press: Oxford, 1980).

DIELS, H., *Die Fragmente der Vorsokratiker*, 6th edn. (3 vols.; Weidmannsche Verlagsbuchhandlung: Berlin-Grunewald, 1951–2).

DUMMETT, M., 'A Defence of McTaggart's Proof of the Unreality of Time', in *Truth and Other Enigmas* (Duckworth: London, 1978).

EMMET, D., *The Effectiveness of Causes* (Macmillan: London and Basingstoke, 1984).

FERBER, R., *Zenons Paradoxien der Bewegung und die Struktur von Raum und Zeit* (Beck: Munich, 1981).

FLOOD, R., and LOCKWOOD, M. (eds.), *The Nature of Time* (Basil Blackwell: Oxford, 1986).

FREEMAN, K., *Ancilla to the Pre-Socratic Philosophers. A Complete Translation of the Fragments in Diels, Die Fragmente der Vorsokratiker.*

GEACH, P. T., *Logic Matters* (Basil Blackwell: Oxford, 1972).

—— *Truth, Love and Immortality: An Introduction to McTaggart's Philosophy* (Hutchinson: London, 1979).

—— 'What Actually Exists', *Proceedings of the Aristotelian Society*, supplementary volume 42 (1968), 7–16.

GELLNER, E., *Thought and Change* (Weidenfeld and Nicholson: London, 1964).

GÖDEL, K., 'A Remark about the Relationship between Relativity Theory and Idealistic Philosophy', in P. A. Schilpp (ed.), *Albert Einstein, Philosopher-Scientist* (Harper & Brothers: New York, 1959).

GRÜNBAUM, A., *Modern Science and Zeno's Paradoxes* (George Allen and Unwin: London, 1968).

HEGEL, G. W. F., *Logic*, trans. W. Wallace (Clarendon Press: Oxford, 1975).

—— *The Phenomenology of Mind*, trans. J. L. Baillie (George Allen and Unwin: London, 1971).

HEISENBERG, W., *Der Teil und das Ganze* (Deutscher Taschenbuch Verlag: Munich, 1973).

HINCKFUSS, I., *The Existence of Space and Time* (Clarendon Press: Oxford, 1975).

HUME, D., *A Treatise of Human Nature* (Clarendon Press: Oxford, 1964).

KANT, I., *Immanuel Kant's Critique of Pure Reason*, trans. N. Kemp-Smith (Macmillan: London, 1964).

KIRK, G. S., RAVEN, J. E., and SCHOFIELD, M., *The Presocratic Philosophers*, 2nd edn. (Cambridge University Press: Cambridge, 1983).

KLINE, A. D., 'Humean Causation and the Necessity of Temporal Discontinuity', *Mind*, 94 (Oct. 1985), 550–6.

LEE,. H. D. P., *Zeno of Elea* (Cambridge University Press: Cambridge, 1936).

LEIBNIZ, G. W., *New Essays on Human Understanding*, trans. P. Remnant and J. Bennett (Cambridge University Press: Cambridge, 1981).

LLOYD, A. C., *Form and Universal in Aristotle* (Francis Cairns: Liverpool, 1981).

LOMBARD, L. B., *Events: A Metaphysical Study* (Routledge and Kegan Paul: London, Boston, and Henley, 1986).

MCTAGGART, J. E., 'The Unreality of Time', *Mind*, 17 (Oct. 1908), 457–74.

MALCOLM, N., 'Memory and the Past', in *Knowledge and Certainty* (Prentice-Hall: Englewood Cliffs, NJ, 1963).

MELLOR, D. H., *Real Time* (Cambridge University Press: Cambridge, 1981).

MOURELATOS, A. P. D. (ed.), *The Pre-Socratics* (Anchor Press: New York, 1974).

NAGEL, E., 'Teleological Explanation', in J. V. Canfield (ed.), *Purpose in Nature* (Prentice-Hall: Englewood Cliffs, NJ, 1966).

NEWTON-SMITH, W. H., *The Structure of Time* (Routledge and Kegan Paul: London, 1980).

OWENS, J., *The Doctrine of Being in the Aristotelian* Metaphysics, 3rd edn. (Pontifical Institute of Mediaeval Studies: Toronto, 1978).

PIVČEVIĆ, E., *The Concept of Reality* (Duckworth: London, 1986).

PLATO, *Parmenides*, trans. F. M. Cornford, in *The Collected Dialogues of Plato*, ed. E. Hamilton and H. Cairns (Princeton University Press: Princeton, NJ, 1973).

PLOTINUS, with English trans. by A. H. Armstrong (7 vols.; Heinemann: Cambridge, Mass. and London, 1966), vol. v, Ennead v. 5.

PROCLUS, *Commentary on Plato's* Parmenides, trans. G. R. Morrow and J. M. Dillon (Princeton University Press: Princeton, NJ, 1987).

QUINTON, A. M. 'Spaces and Times', *Philosophy*, 37 (1962), 130–47.

ROBINSON, A., *Non-Standard Analysis* (North Holland: Amsterdam and London, 1970).

SEXTUS EMPIRICUS, *Against the Physicists*, in *Sextus Empiricus*, with English trans. by R. G. Bury, iii (Heinemann: London and Cambridge, Mass., 1936).

SMITH, J. M. (ed.), · *Evolution Now* (*Nature*, in association with Macmillan: London and Basingstoke, 1982).

STOKES, M. C., *One and Many in Presocratic Philosophy* (Center for Hellenistic Studies: Washington, 1971).

THOMPSON, I. J., 'Real Dispositions in the Physical World', *British Journal for the Philosophy of Science*, 39 (1988), 67–79.

TUGENDHAT, E., *Self-Consciousness and Self-Determination*, trans. P. Stern (MIT Press: Cambridge, Mass., 1986).

WALLACE, W. A., *Causality and Scientific Explanation*, 2 vols. (University of Michigan Press: Ann Arbor, 1972–4).

WATERLOW, S., *Nature, Change, and Agency in Aristotle's Physics* (Clarendon Press: Oxford, 1982).

WHITEHEAD, A. N., *The Concept of Nature* (Cambridge University Press: Cambridge, 1964).

INDEX